EVALUATION OF PARENTING CAPACITY IN CHILD PROTECTION

BEST PRACTICES IN FORENSIC MENTAL HEALTH ASSESSMENT

Series Editors

Thomas Grisso, Alan M. Goldstein, and Kirk Heilbrun

Series Advisory Board

Paul Appelbaum, Richard Bonnie, and John Monahan

Titles in the Series

Foundations of Forensic Mental Health Assessment, *Kirk Heilbrun, Thomas Grisso, and Alan M. Goldstein*

Criminal Titles

Evaluation of Competence to Stand Trial, *Patricia A. Zapf and Ronald Roesch*

Evaluation of Criminal Responsibility, *Ira K. Packer*

Evaluating Capacity to Waive Miranda Rights, *Alan M. Goldstein and Naomi E. Sevin Goldstein*

Evaluation of Sexually Violent Predators, *Philip H. Witt and Mary Alice Conroy*

Evaluation for Risk of Violence in Adults, *Kirk Heilbrun*

Jury Selection, *Margaret Bull Kovera and Brian L. Cutler*

Evaluation for Capital Sentencing, *Mark D. Cunningham*

Eyewitness Identification, *Brian L. Cutler and Margaret Bull Kovera*

Civil Titles

Evaluation of Capacity to Consent to Treatment and Research, *Scott Y. H. Kim*

Evaluation for Guardianship, *Eric Y. Drogin and Curtis L. Barrett*

Evaluation for Personal Injury Claims, *Andrew W. Kane and Joel Dvoskin*

Evaluation for Civil Commitment, *Debra Pinals and Douglas Mossman*

Evaluation for Workplace Discrimination and Harassment, *William Foote and Jane Goodman-Delahunty*

Evaluation of Workplace Disability, *Lisa D. Piechowski*

Juvenile and Family Titles

Evaluation for Child Custody, *Geri S.W. Fuhrmann*

Evaluation of Juveniles' Competence to Stand Trial, *Ivan Kruh and Thomas Grisso*

Evaluation for Risk of Violence in Juveniles, *Robert Hoge and D.A. Andrews*

Evaluation of Parenting Capacity in Child Protection, *Karen S. Budd, Mary Connell, and Jennifer R. Clark*

Evaluation for Disposition and Transfer of Juvenile Offenders, *Randall T. Salekin*

EVALUATION OF PARENTING CAPACITY IN CHILD PROTECTION

KAREN S. BUDD

MARY CONNELL

JENNIFER R. CLARK

OXFORD
UNIVERSITY PRESS

Oxford University Press, Inc., publishes works that further
Oxford University's objective of excellence
in research, scholarship, and education.

Oxford New York
Auckland   Cape Town   Dar es Salaam   Hong Kong   Karachi
Kuala Lumpur   Madrid   Melbourne   Mexico City   Nairobi
New Delhi   Shanghai   Taipei Toronto

With offices in
Argentina   Austria   Brazil   Chile   Czech Republic   France   Greece
Guatemala   Hungary   Italy   Japan   Poland   Portugal   Singapore
South Korea   Switzerland   Thailand   Turkey   Ukraine   Vietnam

Published by Oxford University Press, Inc.
198 Madison Avenue, New York, New York 10016
www.oup.com

Library of Congress Cataloging-in-Publication Data

Budd, Karen S.
Evaluation of parenting capacity in child protection / Karen S. Budd,
Jennifer Clark, Mary A. Connell.
p. cm. — (Best practices in forensic mental health assessment)
Includes bibliographical references and index.
ISBN 978-0-19-533360-2
1. Forensic psychiatry. 2. Child welfare. I. Clark, Jennifer.
II. Connell, Mary A. III. Title. IV. Series.

RA1151.B915 2011
614'.15—dc22   2010028073

About *Best Practices in Forensic Mental Health Assessment*

The recent growth of the fields of forensic psychology and forensic psychiatry has created a need for this book series describing best practices in forensic mental health assessment (FMHA). Currently, forensic evaluations are conducted by mental health professionals for a variety of criminal, civil, and juvenile legal questions. The research foundation supporting these assessments has become broader and deeper in recent decades. Consensus has become clearer on the recognition of essential requirements for ethical and professional conduct. In the larger context of the current emphasis on "empirically supported" assessment and intervention in psychiatry and psychology, the specialization of FMHA has advanced sufficiently to justify a series devoted to best practices. Although this series focuses mainly on evaluations conducted by psychologists and psychiatrists, the fundamentals and principles offered also apply to evaluations conducted by clinical social workers, psychiatric nurses, and other mental health professionals.

This series describes "best practice" as empirically supported (when the relevant research is available), legally relevant, and consistent with applicable ethical and professional standards. Authors of the books in this series identify the approaches that seem best, while incorporating what is practical and acknowledging that "best practice" represents a goal the forensic clinician should aspire to, rather than a standard that can always be met. The American Academy of Forensic Psychology assisted the editors in enlisting the consultation of board-certified forensic psychologists specialized in each topic area. Board-certified forensic psychiatrists were also consultants on many of the volumes. Their comments on the manuscripts helped ensure that the methods described in these volumes represent a generally accepted view of best practice.

The series' authors were selected for their specific expertise in a particular area. At the broadest level, however, certain general principles apply to all types of forensic evaluations. Rather than repeat those fundamental principles in every volume, the series offers them in the first volume, *Foundations of Forensic Mental Health Assessment*. Reading the first book, followed by a specific topical book, will provide the reader both the general principles that the specific topic shares with all forensic evaluations and those that are particular to the specific assessment question.

The specific topics of the 19 books were selected by the series editors as the most important and oft-considered areas of forensic assessment conducted by mental health professionals and behavioral scientists. Each of the 19 topical books is organized according to a common template. The authors address the applicable legal context, forensic mental health concepts, and empirical foundations and limits in the "Foundation" part of the book. They then describe preparation for the evaluation, data collection, data interpretation, and report writing and testimony in the "Application" part of the book. This creates a fairly uniform approach to considering these areas across different topics. All authors in this series have attempted to be as concise as possible in addressing best practice in their area. In addition, topical volumes feature elements to make them user-friendly in actual practice. These elements include boxes that highlight especially important information, relevant case law, best-practice guidelines, and cautions against common pitfalls. A glossary of key terms is also provided in each volume.

We hope the series will be useful for different groups of individuals. Practicing forensic clinicians will find succinct, current information relevant to their practice. Those who are in training to specialize in forensic mental health assessment (whether in formal training or in the process of re-specialization) should find helpful the combination of broadly applicable considerations presented in the first volume together with the more specific aspects of other volumes in the series. Those who teach and supervise trainees can offer these volumes as a guide for practices to which the trainee can aspire. Researchers and scholars interested in FMHA best practice may find researchable ideas, particularly on topics that have received insufficient research attention to date. Judges and attorneys with questions about FMHA best practice will find these books relevant and concise. Clinical and forensic administrators who run agencies, court clinics, and hospitals in which litigants are assessed may also use some of the books in this series to establish expectations for evaluations performed by professionals in their agencies.

We also anticipate that the 19 specific books in this series will serve as reference works that will help courts and attorneys evaluate the quality of forensic mental health professionals' evaluations. A word of caution is in order, however. These volumes focus on best practice, not on what is minimally acceptable legally or ethically. Courts involved in malpractice litigation, or ethics committees or licensure boards considering complaints, should not expect that materials describing best practice easily or necessarily translate into the minimally acceptable professional conduct that is typically at issue in such proceedings.

The present volume, *Evaluation of Parenting Capacity in Child Protection Matters*, focuses on a legal arena in which forensic mental examiners play a delicate and important role. Few values are more respected in Western society than the sanctity of the relationship between parents and their children. Society does not disturb this relationship except under extraordinary circumstances. Among those circumstances are abuse and neglect of the child by the parent.

In such cases, mental health examiners play a crucial role. They assess the needs of the child, the capacities of parents to meet those needs, and the potential consequences of allowing the relationship to continue. And they advise the court regarding its decision about the potential need for temporary suspension or permanent termination of parental rights. This is a highly specialized type of evaluation, requiring child clinical specialization, a knowledge of the legal and social context, and a thorough understanding of the professional and ethical guidelines for child-protection evaluations. This volume provides the foundation that any mental health professional needs when pursuing specialization in evaluating parents before the court in child abuse and neglect cases.

Thomas Grisso
Kirk Heilbrun
Alan M. Goldstein

Acknowledgments

Writing this book has been a journey of learning and collaboration for us. Although we came to the subject of parenting in child protection cases along different paths, we share a passionate interest in the complicated issues surrounding the assessment of minimal parenting competence. The opportunity to write this book has provided us the occasion for numerous thought-provoking debates and discussions on scholarly, clinical, and practical questions we have encountered in evaluating parents. We brought our experiences to bear on shaping a book that, we hope, will be helpful to professionals tackling these challenging assessments. In the process, we learned a great deal from each other and from the literature that has informed our commentary. We expect that readers will have much to offer us from their experiences, and we invite their comments and suggestions.

The authors gratefully acknowledge the important contributions made by Kathryn Kuehnle early in the project. Dr. Kuehnle's guidance and direction got the volume underway and was of great assistance in shaping the final project. We also thank the series editors Kirk Heilbrun, Thomas Grisso, and Alan Goldstein for inviting and supporting us in writing this book. In particular, we have benefited from the editorial guidance and support of Dr. Grisso, as our manuscript editor, throughout the writing process. His measured and discerning comments on the chapter drafts sharpened our thinking and improved our writing. We are also grateful to Oxford University Press for sponsoring this series and our volume. Regan Hofmann, Christina Wojdyjo, and others at Oxford have been very helpful in moving this book through the editorial process. We also appreciate the positive feedback and helpful suggestions of our outside reviewer, Marsha Hedrick.

Each of us is indebted to individuals who served as mentors and colleagues in forensic assessment prior to and during the preparation of this volume. Karen Budd extends sincere thanks to the staff of the Clinical Evaluation and Services Initiative of Cook County Juvenile Court, particularly to Julie Biehl, Barbara Kahn, Amy Anson, Joe Scally, and Dana Baerger, for honing her thinking on the thorny issues of assessing parents in a forensic context. Mary Connell thanks Randy Otto, Kathryn Kuehnle, and Eric Drogin for their ongoing contributions to her professional development, and Karen Budd for the excellent research and writing she has contributed to the field that has enlightened all forensic practitioners who work in child maltreatment matters. Jennifer Clark would like to thank Karen Budd for the opportunity to collaborate on this volume and for the invaluable insights she has offered during the years of working together. Jennifer also extends sincere thanks to her former and current colleagues at the Cook County Juvenile Court Clinic for their support and encouragement as this volume came to fruition. In addition, we especially thank our families for their dedication, patience, and support. We acknowledge with gratitude Karen's husband Ben Friedman and son Jacob, Mary's husband, Michael Heymann, and Jennifer's husband Tom and son Nathan for their patience with the time we devoted to writing.

Contents

EVALUATION OF PARENTING CAPACITY IN CHILD PROTECTION

FOUNDATION

The Legal Context   1

W hen parenting comes into question due to child abuse or neglect, caseworkers, attorneys, and judges often turn to mental health professionals for expert guidance. Child protection evaluations may be requested for information regarding a parent's caregiving capacities, risk and protective factors associated with placement or visitation, a child's emotional or psychological needs, or intervention strategies that may assist parenting or child development. Evaluations may be requested at various points and may serve different functions depending on when they are requested. The overarching question in child protection evaluations is, "What is in the child's best interest?" but the specific focus varies with the referral concerns; for example, "What are the mental health needs of the parent, and how do they impact the child?" "What intervention strategies may work best to address the parent's alleged deficits?" or "What effect will *termination of parental rights* have on this child?"

This volume addresses issues and methods of forensic mental health assessment (FMHA) of parents and the parent–child relationship in child protection matters. Assessment of the child will be addressed when relevant in the context of assessing parental caregiving capabilities; however, the primary focus of the book is on parenting capacity evaluations. In this volume, the terms *evaluation* and *assessment* are used interchangeably.

The history of child protection and the legal context for child protection assessments are addressed in this chapter. In Chapter 2, the legal concepts are translated into forensic mental health concepts to form the foundation for assessment. In Chapter 3, the empirical research undergirding the assessment is reviewed, with summaries of relevant research on parents in child protection matters and on assessment methods relevant to this population. Chapters 4 through 7 describe the assessment process, with discussion of preparation (Chapter 4), data collection and interpretation (Chapters 5 and 6), and report writing and testimony (Chapter 7).

Rights of Parents and Society's Responsibility to Protect Children

Respect for parental rights and authority has long been recognized as a tenet of society. A brief historical perspective is first provided here by considering how our courts have dealt with parental rights and child protection and how society has structured child protective services.

A Brief History of Parental Rights in the Courts

Courts are loath to usurp parental rights. Several early Supreme Court decisions held that the Fourteenth Amendment protects the fundamental liberty of parents to make decisions regarding their children. *Pierce v. Society of Sisters* (1925) asserted parental rights to direct their children's education when a state (Oregon) sought to compel parents to send their 8- to 16-year-old children to public school. In *Meyer v. Nebraska* (1923), the high court articulated the right to parent as one of the fundamental privileges. It found a Nebraska law prohibiting teaching a child a foreign language to be a violation of due process rights to:

> ...engage in any of the common occupations of life, to acquire useful knowledge, to marry, establish a home and bring up children, to worship God according to the dictates of his own conscience, and generally to enjoy those privileges long recognized at common law as essential to the orderly pursuit of happiness by free men. (p. 399)

Similarly, *Griswold v. Connecticut* (1965) recognized the right to enjoy the mutual care, company, love, and affection of one's children, a right that could not be taken away without due process of law. Since these early decisions, the Supreme Court has dealt with numerous petitions to interpret state laws restricting the

CASE LAW

*Pierce v. Society of
Sisters*, 1925

● One of several
early Supreme Court
decisions that significantly
expanded coverage of the
Due Process Clause in the
Fourteenth Amendment.

● The U.S. Supreme Court
held that the Oregon
Compulsory Education Act
of 1922 violated parents'
rights to direct the education
of their children

rights of parents to unfettered access, care, and control of their children.

Set against this backdrop regarding the right to parent one's children is another value, a generally recognized responsibility of society to protect its children. The doctrine of *parens patriae*, or "country [nation] as parent," recognizes that government has a strong interest in the care and nurturing of children and others who cannot function independently (Otto & Melton, 1990). Laws pertaining to the custody of children and termination of parental rights have arisen because society assumes the responsibility to protect children when families are disrupted or seriously dysfunctional. In *Prince v. Massachusetts* (1944), the Supreme Court held that the government has broad authority to regulate the actions and treatment of children, noting that parental authority is not absolute and can be permissibly restricted if doing so advances the interests of a child's welfare. However, "It is cardinal with us that the custody, care and nurturance of the child reside first in the parents, whose primary function and freedom include preparation for obligations the state can neither supply nor hinder" (p. 166).

The U.S. Supreme Court decided in *Santosky v. Kramer* (1982) that "clear and convincing evidence," rather than a less demanding "preponderance of evidence," was necessary when the state sought to terminate a parent's rights. The high court determined that the fundamental liberty interest of natural parents in the care, custody, and management of their child is protected by the Fourteenth Amendment. That interest does not "evaporate simply because they have not been model parents or have lost

- The Supreme
  Court held that the
  government has broad
  authority to regulate the
  actions and treatment of
  children.

- It also held that parental
  authority is not absolute and
  can be permissibly restricted
  if doing so advances the
  interests of a child's welfare.

temporary custody of their child to the State . . . parents retain a vital interest in preventing the irretrievable destruction of their family life" (p.753).

The Supreme Court once again considered the sanctity and breadth of parents' rights to determine what is in their children's best interests in *Troxel et vir v. Granville* (2000), a case involving grandparents' challenge to their daughter-in-law's refusal to allow them visitation with their granddaughters after their son (the children's father) died. The Supreme Court, noting that strict scrutiny must occur when the state seeks to intervene in parents' rights, refused the grandparents' request for the visitation that the mother did not want to allow. The Washington statute permitting the court to grant visitation to anyone if the court deemed it would serve the children's best interests was determined by the Supreme Court to violate parents' rights to rear their children as they saw fit. Reasoning that the Constitution permits a state to interfere with this right only to prevent harm or potential harm to the child, the Supreme Court found that the Washington statute represented a threat to parental rights.

CASE LAW

Santosky v. Kramer,
1982

- The Court
  decided that the state may
  only terminate parental
  rights by showing "clear and
  convincing" evidence.

- This changed the standard,
  which was, in some states,
  "fair preponderance."

However, the Supreme Court continues to defer to states to establish and maintain appropriate balancing tests between the state's role, as *parens patriae*, to look after the welfare of children in need and the parents' constitutional rights to the care and control of their children. Recently, the Supreme Court, petitioned to review

CASE LAW
Troxel et vir v.
Granville, 2000

- The U.S. Supreme Court held that parents have a constitutional right to rear their children as they see fit.

- The decision struck down a Washington state law that allowed any third party to petition state courts for child visitation rights over parental objections.

the power of the state to require cooperation from parents under investigation for alleged abuse, declined to review a challenge to Illinois' Safety Plan (*Dupuy v. McEwen*, 2008). The basis for challenge was that when an allegation of abuse or neglect is made, no matter how potentially frivolous, the state can require parents to agree to a safety plan or face removal of the child. The safety plan may require one parent to move out of the home and have limited or no contact with a child for months while the state conducts an investigation. The state has no burden of a particular standard of proof.

Thus, tension between states' obligations as *parens patriae* and parental autonomy will continue to arise, and the Supreme Court may continue to decline review in favor of state autonomy to regulate that tension. States enjoy considerable latitude in fulfilling the function of *parens patriae*, and parents who object to their state's intrusion have an uphill battle to be heard by the higher court.

History of Child Protection Services

Society has evolved in its appreciation for its responsibility to protect children. The history is a sordid one. In the early eighteenth century, children whose parents could not care for them were often cast out to make their own way and might live on the streets, begging for food, or in almshouses with poverty-stricken adults (Myers, 2006). There they might be exploited, mistreated, or even beaten. By mid-century, there was some recognition of the needs of these children, and the first orphanages were established, yet

INFO
The U.S. Supreme Court tends to defer to states in child protection cases.

conditions for the children were often deplorable (Myers, 2004). These children were considered to have a status of almost less than human. In the late 1800s, one such child, known then only as "Mary Ellen," was brought to the attention of the authorities because of alleged abuse by her foster parents. The influence her case wrought on the social services offered to maltreated children has become legendary, and for that reason, it is interesting to explore her history.

In 1874, a Methodist mission worker, Etta Angell Wheeler, took up the cause of Mary Ellen (American Humane Society, n.d.), a 10-year-old girl who was being severely abused and neglected by her New York foster parents. Frustrated by the reluctance of New York City authorities to enforce existing laws that prohibited excessive physical discipline of children, Ms. Wheeler sought the assistance of Henry Bergh, president of the New York Society for the Prevention of Cruelty to Animals. Mr. Bergh, acting as a concerned citizen, assisted in obtaining relief for Mary Ellen, and the case became widely regarded as a shameful exposé of the scandal of children having less protection under the law than animals. While it was actually not the law protecting animals that was applied in Mary Ellen's case, it was indeed Mr. Bergh's official role and expertise in working within the governmental system and the press that provided for the rescue of Mary Ellen and the development of a formalized child protection system (Watkins, 1990). Out of the publicity of the case came the eventual development of the Society for the Prevention of Cruelty to Children, and by 1950 there were 480 such groups in the United States (New York Society for the Prevention of Cruelty to Children, 2000).

The care and protection of children remained primarily a family matter, however, with limited state oversight, until the early 1960s (Myers, 2004). A number of factors brought increasing attention to child maltreatment cases, and, during the following two decades, remarkable

INFO

The legendary case of foster child Mary Ellen Wilson in the late 1800s led to the development of a formalized child protection system in the United States.

advances occurred to coordinate intervention when children were in need of protection. Kempe and colleagues (1962) introduced the term *battered child syndrome,* heightening awareness within the medical community of the plight of the severely abused or neglected children who sometimes came to the attention of doctors. Television no doubt raised community consciousness of the existence of severe abuse, widely publicizing the work of Kempe and colleagues (1962) on the phenomenon of child battering and of dangers children might face in their own homes (Myers, 2004).

Governmental attention to the problem increased through the establishment of the National Institute on Child Health and Human Development in 1963. Funding was made available for broad implementation of preventive intervention and for response to existing cases of abuse and neglect through the passage of the landmark Child Abuse Prevention and Treatment Act of 1974 (CAPTA, 1974). As described further in the next section, CAPTA also encouraged states to enact legislation to mandate the reporting of child abuse and neglect, further fueling public awareness and highlighting the need for governmental response (Myers, 2004). The response could include investigation, provision of in-home and foster care services to help parents meet parenting challenges and remedy deficits, and, when remediation was not possible, termination of parental rights and placement for adoption.

As states developed both statutes and intervention strategies to deal with child maltreatment, "child welfare" offices were established in most densely populated areas. Through the years, alternative titles have been adopted for these agencies, sometimes reflecting the department within which the child protection agency existed, such as the Department of Human Services (DHS), Department of Health and Social Services (DHSS), Department of Child and Family Services (DCFS), or the Department of Social Services (DSS). The generic term *Child Protective Services* (CPS) is easily understood and, for the purposes of economy, is used in this volume to refer to any state's agency that investigates and provides services when child maltreatment is suspected.

Federal Legislation Affecting Child Protection

Over three decades have passed since the first federal child protection act became law, and social policy has been shaped by, and has further influenced, this legislation. A detailed analysis of the nature of that influence is beyond the scope of this volume (see, e.g., Guggenheim, 1995; Jimenez, 1990; Rosenfeld et al., 1994), but a brief review of the general nature of the legislation is helpful to illuminate the context in which child protection evaluations occur.

Child Abuse Prevention and Treatment Act (CAPTA)

Several federal Acts have provided direction and funding to states for child protection. These Acts have provided minimum standards for defining child physical abuse and neglect and sexual abuse that states must incorporate into their statutory definitions in order to receive federal funds. In 1974, the initial Child Abuse Prevention and Treatment Act provided funding to states to prevent, identify, and treat child abuse and neglect. CAPTA required states, for federal funding, to adopt laws requiring mandatory reporting to authorities of suspected child abuse, to ensure confidentiality of agency records and court proceedings, and to appoint a guardian *ad litem* for every child in maltreatment proceedings. The focus then was on protecting children and making sure they did not fall between the bureaucratic cracks as state agencies intervened on their behalf.

INFO

Passed in 1974, CAPTA sets forth a minimum definition of "child abuse and neglect" and provides federal funding to states in support of prevention, assessment, investigation, prosecution, and treatment activities.

Social Services Block Grant, Title XX

Social Services Amendments of 1974 added a new title to the Social Security Act: Title XX. The Social Services Block Grant, Title XX of the Social Security Act (1975), provided funding for, among other things, child protection including prevention, treatment programs, and foster care and adoption services. The block grant authorized grants to states for the purpose of "preventing or remedying neglect, abuse, or exploitation of children . . . unable to protect their own interests, or preserving, rehabilitating, or reuniting families" (Sec. 2001 [3]). Specific services it aimed to fund that fell under the umbrella of "child welfare" were emergency shelter care; protective services for children; services for children in foster care; information, referral, and counseling services; services designed to meet the special needs of children, individuals with developmental disabilities, and those with substance-abuse problems; and child care. Funds were aimed at the needs of low-income families and individuals.

Indian Child Welfare Act (ICWA)

The Indian Child Welfare Act, enacted in 1978 (ICWA, P.L. 95-608), provided specific protections to American Indian families. ICWA required states to provide specific protections to American Indian children in maltreatment and juvenile proceedings. ICWA established the right of the tribe to intervene or to petition for transfer to tribal court. It standardized practices for removing American Indian children from their homes. The Act also established a protocol of preferences for placement of children removed from their homes, giving priority to family members, tribe members, and other American Indians. It directed agencies to engage in "active efforts" to reunify families and clarified jurisdictional rights of American Indian tribes in relation to their children. ICWA provided for grants for on- and off-reservation American Indian child and family programs.

Adoption Assistance and Child Welfare Act (AACWA) and Family Preservation and Support Initiative

The Adoption Assistance and Child Welfare Act (AACWA, 1980), intended to assist the states in protecting and caring for abused and neglected children, required funded states to serve children in their own homes, prevent out-of-home placement, and facilitate family reunification following placement. AACWA established a strong preference for the child's biological family as the permanency option and provided protocols for reimbursing some foster care and adoption costs. AACWA established case plan requirements, out-of-home placement directives, guidelines for voluntary placement, and timelines for court reviews and hearings. The rights of parents were protected through oversight and regulation of child welfare programs. AACWA prioritized reunification as the preferred permanency outcome.

The Family Preservation and Support Initiative (1993) also supported family preservation by funding services that were intended to assist vulnerable children and families prior to any maltreatment, and funding family preservation services to help families resolve crises that would otherwise lead to foster care for their children.

The emphasis in these early Acts was on in-home intervention and the judicious use of foster and adoptive placement. Concern arose in the child protection community, however, that the "reasonable efforts" requirement of AACWA meant that child welfare agencies were obligated to return children to unsafe homes (Youth Law Center, 2000). A modification of AACWA in 1997 articulated exceptions to the "reasonable efforts" requirement and obligated states to ensure that children would not languish in foster care when reunification efforts failed or were not practicable. Beginning in the late 1990s, federal legislation subtly shifted to increasingly emphasize seeking permanency for children who must be removed from their homes for their protection from maltreatment—as described next.

Adoption and Safe Families Act (ASFA)

A change in the thrust of intervention occurred with passage of the Adoption and Safe Families Act (ASFA, P.L. 105.89, 1997), modifying AACWA. This Act changed the name from the "Family Preservation and Support Initiative" to "Promoting Safe and Stable Families" and required states to move foster children more rapidly into permanent homes by terminating parental rights more quickly and by encouraging adoptions. ASFA established

INFO

The Adoption Assistance and Child Welfare Act of 1980 was interpreted by states as requiring biological families be kept together no matter what.

a timeline and conditions for filing for termination of parental rights. Whereas previously, states may have waited until the court made a determination regarding termination of parental rights to begin planning for adoption, ASFA required states to begin, concurrent with the petition to terminate parental rights, to seek an adoptive placement for any child in foster care for 15 of the most recent 22 months.

ASFA also required states to file a termination petition on behalf of abandoned infants or when a parent of a child had assaulted the child, or killed or assaulted another one of their children. Exceptions, however, were identified: when the state had made a relative placement; made a compelling case why filing was not in the child's best interest; or had not provided the services deemed necessary to return the child to a safe home. ASFA also shortened the time by which a permanency hearing must occur for a child in out-of-home care, from 18 months to within 12 months of a child's entry into care.

Importantly, as noted earlier, ASFA modified the "reasonable efforts" provision in AACWA. The requirement that states make reasonable efforts to preserve and reunify families was continued, but, in making decisions about the removal of a child from, and the child's return to, his or her home, the child's health and safety were to be the paramount concerns. The "reasonable efforts" requirement does not apply, ASFA established, in cases in which a court has found that the child has been tortured, chronically abused, or sexually abused; the parent has committed murder or solicited murder of another child to the parent; the parent has committed felony assault resulting in serious injury to one of the children; or the parental rights to a sibling have been involuntarily terminated. In these cases, states are not required to make reasonable efforts to preserve or reunify the family. Instead, states must hold a permanency hearing within 30 days and make reasonable efforts to place the child for adoption, with a legal guardian, or in another permanent placement. Thus, the Act obligated child welfare agencies to make reasonable efforts to place a child for adoption or with a legal guardian at the same time as they made efforts to reunify families (Youth Law Center, 2000).

ASFA also required that a foster parent, preadoptive parent, or relative caring for a child be given notice of, and an opportunity to be heard in, any review or hearing involving the child. This provision did not require that any foster or preadoptive parent or relative be made a party to such a review or hearing, but, by being noticed, these concerned caregivers could offer the court important information about how the child dealt with parental visitation, how the child had adapted to care, and what the caregiver anticipated the outcome of various court determinations might be. The impact of this requirement might be substantial, then, both in informing the court of the child's needs but also in detracting from consideration of the parent's legitimate position (Roberts, 2002). ASFA's requirement that the court hear evidence offered by caregivers or potential future caregivers opened the possibility that the court would make comparative judgments between a potentially minimally adequate parent (the parent fighting to retain parental rights) and the hand-selected substitute caregiver (foster, preadoptive, or relative parental figure). Although it was supported by children's advocates, parents' rights advocates expressed concern that the law would result in a subtle shift away from "minimally adequate parenting" to "best available parent." On its face, this provision appears to simply address the child's best interest; however, it may encroach on the rights of those well-intentioned but impoverished, uneducated, or marginally adequate parents whose actions have brought them to the state's attention (Roberts, 2002).

INFO

The Adoption and Safe Families Act was enacted in an attempt to correct problems that stemmed from the Adoption Assistance and Child Welfare Act of 1980. ASFA shifted the emphasis toward children's health and safety concerns and away from a policy of reuniting children with their birth parents without regard to prior abusiveness.

Keeping Children and Families Safe Act (KCFSA)

The Keeping Children and Families Safe Act (KCFSA) (2003, P. L. 108-36) modified CAPTA by requiring that states have procedures to address the needs of drug-exposed infants and triage procedures for the referral of children not at imminent risk of harm to community or preventative services. KCFSA also established the requirement that states have procedures to advise an individual who is the subject of an investigation about the allegations made against them. CPS workers must receive training regarding their legal duties and parents' rights. There must be provisions to refer children under age three who are involved in substantiated cases of abuse or neglect to early intervention services. KCFSA established flexibility for states to determine open-court policies for cases of child abuse and neglect. It provided support and enhancement of interagency collaboration between the child protection system and the juvenile justice system, including methods for continuity of treatment for children who move between the two systems.

Over the past 30 years, then, an emphasis on prevention and in-home services in support of remediation has somewhat given way to a focus on investigation of abuse and swift protective action. Although reunification remains the default goal, remedial intervention has been displaced, to some extent, by foreshortened intervention and termination of parental rights to move children from abusive situations into adoption.

Legal Definitions of Child Maltreatment

In cases of alleged maltreatment, the questions that face the child protective agency and the court are whether a child is in need of protection and whether a parent is responsible for the harm or danger. Following substantiation of child maltreatment, the questions focus on whether the parent is capable of providing minimally adequate parenting to protect the child's safety and well-being. *Child maltreatment* is defined to include physical abuse of a child; child neglect, endangerment, or abandonment; emotional abuse of a child; or child sexual abuse or exploitation. CAPTA (1974) provided working definitions of physical abuse, child neglect, endangerment, abandonment, emotional abuse, sexual abuse, and exploitation that may serve as a starting point, although jurisdictional statutes may vary (see Table 1.1).

Table 1.1 | CAPTA Definitions of Abuse and Neglect

CAPTA, as amended by the Keeping Children and Families Safe Act of 2003 (US HSS CB), defines "child abuse and neglect" to include, at a minimum, any recent act or failure to act on the part of a parent or caretaker which results in death, serious physical or emotional harm, sexual abuse or exploitation, or an act or failure to act which presents an imminent risk of serious harm.

- *Physical abuse* is the nonaccidental physical injury to a child including striking, kicking, burning, or biting.

- *Child neglect* is generally defined as deprivation of adequate food, clothing, shelter, or medical care (and the state may distinguish failure to provide based on financial inability from failure to provide for no apparent financial reason).

- *Endangerment* may be defined as placing the child in circumstances or with individuals that could reasonably be expected to put the child at risk of harm or inadequate care. *Abandonment* is leaving the child with no expressed intent to return, or failure to return for a specified time.

- *Emotional abuse* of a child involves injury to the psychological capacity or emotional stability of the child as evidenced by an observable or substantial change in behavior, emotional response, or cognition, or as evidenced by anxiety, depression, withdrawal, or aggressive behavior.

- Statutes related to *sexual abuse and exploitation* of children may be general or may explicate the specific acts considered to be abusive or exploitative. *Sexual abuse* may be defined in terms of motivation (whether touching was for purpose of sexual arousal), and the statute may specify areas touched or the degree of penetration. *Exploitation* generally includes allowing the child to engage in prostitution or involving the child in the production of child pornography (CAPTA, 1974).

The suspicion of abuse or neglect may incur various levels of intervention, such as providing in-home services; temporary removal of the child to a relative placement, foster care, or a group home or residential facility; or plans for termination of parental rights. In each case there may be a request for assessment to address issues at that intervention point. Some forms of abuse, such as over-discipline; some forms of neglect, such as leaving elementary school–aged children unattended; and some forms of emotional abuse may warrant protective in-home intervention and may not be handled in the courts. Nevertheless, an assessment requested in such a case, even for purposes of treatment planning, is a forensic assessment in that the assessment may be compelled and the case may escalate to a legal matter. Forensic assessments in child protection matters are not limited to "termination of parental rights" assessments, as they are sometimes called, and rarely do they begin in a context in which termination of parental rights is considered inevi-

INFO

Intervention for abuse and neglect may include in-home services, removal of the child from the home, or termination of parental rights. Forensic assessment may be requested for any of these cases.

1
chapter

table (Melton et al., 2007). Instead, they often are requested at earlier stages of the case.

Legal Standard: Best Interests of the Child

The idea that society should respect the best interests of the child is seen as fundamental in our culture. Society views children as its most vulnerable citizens and as the embodiment of its future. The legal decision-maker (usually a judge) must determine what is in the child's best interests. This decision was once guided by the notion of children being "chattel" or possessions of the parent, and thus generally of the father, who was in English common law the owner of all property of the marriage (Mason, 1994). By the end of the nineteenth century, courts recognized that children, particularly those of "tender years," might need the care a mother can provide. This *"tender years" doctrine,* which held that mothers were best qualified to care for their children, emerged and for a time prevailed. With shifting views of sex roles and the advent of "no fault" divorce in the 1960s, courts began to discard the tender years presumption. For example, in *State ex rel. Watts v. Watts* (1973), New York's highest court held, "The simple fact of being a mother does not, by itself, indicate a willingness or capacity to render a quality of care different than that which a father can provide." The tender years doctrine has since been replaced with the *best interests of the child standard,* which has been adopted by all jurisdictions in the United States (Otto & Edens, 2003).

Today, *best interests* is defined differently in various state statutes (Child Welfare Information Gateway, 2008), and in some states it is determined by case law. The definition is sufficiently indeterminative (Goldstein, Freud, & Solnit, 1979) to require a case-by-case analysis of what is in the child's best interests. Michigan's Child Custody Act of 1970 serves as a model that reflects many of the elements included in state statutes and is included in the Table 1.2 as an example of how a state might define "best interests."

Generally the concept of best interests is invoked in consideration of contested child custody or access matters in family dissolution. The state statute for best interests may pertain to the comparative strengths of two competing parties vying for the right to be the parent primarily responsible for a child's care. When biological parents are being evaluated for minimally adequate parenting, the state's conceptualization of the child's best interests must be considered without respect to how well the biological parent compares to a foster or potential adoptive parent. The absence of a legal definition of what constitutes minimally adequate parenting, in combination with the focus on the vague legal standard of best interests of the child, may obfuscate this important distinction (Otto & Edens, 2003).

Legal Process: Court Systems Dealing with Children's Rights and Parents' Rights

The maltreatment of a child may be at issue in several kinds of courts. The juvenile dependency[1] court, in which child abuse and neglect cases are tried, hears evidence to determine whether there has been maltreatment and considers the need for protection.

---

1   *Dependency* is used in this volume to refer to civil child abuse and neglect or child protection cases and to courts hearing those cases. The designation "dependency court" is used widely (Summers, Dobbin, & Gatowski, 2008) but not universally across jurisdictions; some less-urban jurisdictions may not have separate dependency courts; and some jurisdictions have "unified family courts" that handle many or all legal proceedings addressing child and family matters (Babb, 2008).

Table 1.2 | Michigan's Child Custody Act of 1970: A Model for Defining the Child's Best Interests

As used in this Act, "best interests of the child" means the sum total of the following factors to be considered, evaluated, and determined by the court:

(a)   The love, affection, and other emotional ties existing between the parties involved and the child.

(b)   The capacity and disposition of the parties involved to give the child love, affection, and guidance and to continue the education and raising of the child in his or her religion or creed, if any.

(c)   The capacity and disposition of the parties involved to provide the child with food, clothing, medical care, or other remedial care recognized and permitted under the laws of this state in place of medical care, and other material needs.

(d)   The length of time the child has lived in a stable, satisfactory environment, and the desirability of maintaining continuity.

(e)   The permanence, as a family unit, of the existing or proposed custodial home or homes.

(f)   The moral fitness of the parties involved.

(g)   The mental and physical health of the parties involved.

(h)   The home, school, and community record of the child.

(i)   The reasonable preference of the child, if the court considers the child to be of sufficient age to express preference.

(j)   The willingness and ability of each of the parties to facilitate and encourage a close and continuing parent–child relationship between the child and the other parent or the child and the parents.

(k)   Domestic violence, regardless of whether the violence was directed against or witnessed by the child.

(l)   Any other factor considered by the court to be relevant to a particular child custody dispute.

Eventually, if maltreating parents cannot be rehabilitated, termination of parental rights is considered in dependency court. The dependency court judge may also finalize later adoption of the child. In family court, where divorce and child custody matters are heard, allegations of child maltreatment may also be raised.

INFO

Child maltreatment may be at issue in any of the following courts:

- Juvenile dependency court
- Family court
- Criminal court
- Civil court

The family court[2] may hear evidence regarding those allegations in determining how to apportion parenting time and responsibility.

Allegations of child abuse or neglect may rise to the level of criminal offenses and be prosecuted in the criminal court system. This legal proceeding may occur contemporaneously with dependency court or family court proceedings. Finally, child maltreatment may constitute a tort action and be litigated in the civil courts where personal injury claims are heard; for example, when abuse was allegedly perpetrated in an institution. Civil litigation often arises years after the maltreatment is alleged to have occurred.

It is possible that a case might be filed in each of the courts and may proceed through litigation in one court after another, serially or simultaneously. For example, allegations of severe neglect by a custodial parent, such as keeping a child locked in a closet throughout the weekends and school holidays, might arise. Investigation by the child protective agency could result in removal of the child and limited or supervised visitation. The noncustodial (and non-neglectful) parent might go to the family court that apportioned parenting responsibility to gain full custody. Criminal charges might also be filed against the neglectful parent. Finally, the non-neglectful parent might sue the school for failing

---

2   *Family court* is used in this volume to refer to civil cases, such as family dissolution matters, in which disputes arise about parenting time or responsibility, In some jurisdictions, juvenile and family court are separate, the former dealing with child protection cases, delinquency, and status offense cases, and the latter dealing with divorce and parenting cases, adoptions, paternity, and domestic violence. The Unified Family Court, being implemented in a number of jurisdictions around the country, has subject-matter jurisdiction over all legal issues related to families and children (see, e.g., Administrative Office of the Courts, American Institutes for Research, 2002). Almost 75% of states now have some form of statewide family court system, and only thirteen states have no specialized system to handle family legal matters (Babb, 2008).

in its duty to report the child's apparent symptoms of severe neglect.

This volume is focused exclusively on dependency court forensic mental health assessment. Evaluations of allegedly maltreated children for family court, civil court, or criminal court proceedings may invoke considerations not addressed here. Dependency evaluations require an appreciation of child protection practices in the jurisdiction, resources for families, and an extensive body of literature concerning child maltreatment.

Legal procedures in dependency court vary from state to state, but there are some general areas of agreement. The CPS system intervenes to provide protection and remediation and, if necessary, to recommend that the court consider terminating parental rights. For the parent, parental competency is at question, and a minimal threshold is generally understood to be required; for the child, the question before the court is best interests—for termination of parental rights, clear and convincing evidence is required. The case may take the following course, as illustrated in Figure 1.1.

Suspicions of abuse or neglect trigger a mandated referral to the state child abuse hotline or directly to a CPS agency. A preliminary investigation is conducted and may result in no action in the absence of evidence that a child is in need of protection. Alternatively, referrals may be made for needed services, followed by case closure. When the alleged abuse or neglect appears to warrant more immediate and intensive services, the case may be opened for in-home ongoing services. In cases of severe or urgent need, the child may be immediately taken into protective custody.

Removal of a child from the parent, even temporarily, is an extreme measure, and the law provides certain protections to ensure that it does not occur capriciously. CPS must file a petition for removal for temporary custody that triggers an initial hearing or emergency hearing. Jurisdictions differ in the terms they use for the initial hearing. It may be called the *preliminary protective hearing, shelter care hearing, detention hearing, emergency removal hearing, show-cause hearing*, or *temporary custody hearing*. This hearing may be held by the juvenile dependency court to determine the need for emergency protection based on preliminary evidence that

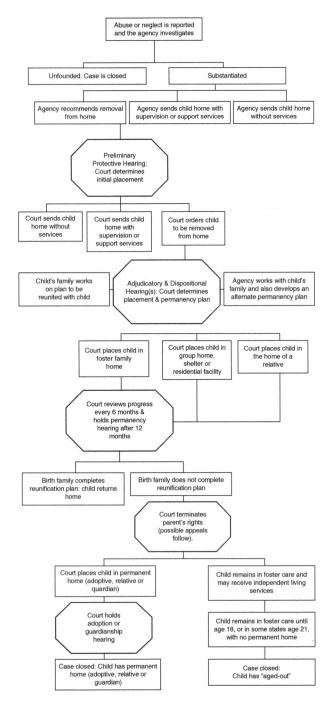

Figure 1.1 A Child's Journey through the Child Protective Services System (Badeau & Gesiriech, 2003, reprinted with permission)

the child may have been a victim of severe maltreatment. This hearing must occur soon after the filing of the petition or the removal of the child. State laws vary in the time provided, but ideally it should occur on the first day following the petition, upon removal of the child, or as soon as possible thereafter. The main purpose is to determine whether the child should be placed in substitute care or remain with or be returned to the parent pending further proceedings. The critical issue is whether in-home placement will put the child at risk (Child Welfare Information Gateway, 2006).

When the alleged abuse or neglect is severe, the case may be simultaneously referred to the local prosecutor for criminal investigation. Hearings and a trial may follow the criminal investigation and may occur alongside the CPS intervention. In some communities, multidisciplinary agencies have been established to coordinate the investigation and, to a limited extent, intervention or treatment for maltreating parents and their children (National Children's Advocacy Center, 2005). Particularly in cases of suspected child sexual abuse, a multidisciplinary agency such as a child advocacy center may combine the investigative efforts of CPS, law enforcement, medical providers, and trained forensic interviewers who coordinate efforts to intervene (Child Welfare Information Gateway, 2006).

Adjudicatory hearings, sometimes called *fact-finding hearings* or *jurisdictional hearings*, occur following the initial proceedings. Their purpose is to determine whether the child has been maltreated or whether some other legal basis exists for the state to intervene to protect the child. Adjudication hearings are followed the same day or within a few weeks by dispositional hearings. At disposition, the court decides whether the child needs services, and orders them, establishes visitation schedules, and, if in-home services are being provided, may order CPS to continue in-home follow-up (Child Welfare Information Gateway, 2006).

Periodic review hearings, status hearings, or progress hearings are held to review whether substitute placement remains a necessity and whether CPS is addressing the child's needs. Review of goals, visitation arrangements, and progress toward reunification are the main legal decisions relevant to parenting capability (Child Welfare Information Gateway, 2006). A final hearing is generally held to formalize return of the child to the parents and cessation of the state's involvement following successful intervention or, when intervention has been unsuccessful, to terminate parental rights. Permanent placement without termination is an option in some states. The court may, at earlier stages in the case, act on "reason to believe" or "preponderance of the evidence" as a basis for ordering protective intervention. For termination of parental rights, however, there must be "clear and convincing" evidence that the statute was met (*Santosky v. Kramer,* 1982) (Child Welfare Information Gateway, 2006).

Summary

Although there are jurisdictional differences in the laws regulating child protection matters and in the names by which legal proceedings are known, there is considerable uniformity across jurisdictions in some respects. The courts continue to grapple with the competing tensions of child protection and parental rights, and the Supreme Court often defers to the state courts' decisions about these matters. Federal Acts requiring state compliance in order to assure ongoing funding have served to standardize, to some extent, the approach taken by various Child Protective Services and by the court systems. Federal legislation has reduced what could otherwise be vast differences in philosophies about removal of children from their parents and differences in practice, for example, with regard to family reunification versus permanency planning and inclusion of foster parents in case planning and disposition. Thus far, there are no federally promulgated standards defining specific types of child maltreatment or what constitutes the "best interests of the child" for protection cases. Likewise, the threshold of "minimally adequate parenting" has not been defined. These concepts, and the translation from concept to the psycholegal question, are the focus of Chapter 2.

Forensic Mental Health Concepts | **2**

Forensic mental health assessment (FMHA) refers to the objective evaluation of psychological phenomena conducted for the court or likely to be used in legal proceedings (Heilbrun, Grisso, & Goldstein, 2009). Whether a child protection evaluation is specifically ordered by the court or is requested by a social service agency, there is a high probability that it will be used in court proceedings. For this reason, the assessment should be conceived differently from a clinical or therapeutic assessment. This chapter describes how FMHAs in child protection differ from assessments for clinical purposes; professional guidelines for FMHA practice in child protection; and frameworks for formulating and answering questions in assessments. It distinguishes between parenting evaluations conducted in child protection and child custody contexts. It also illustrates the intersection between legal questions and mental health assessment by considering how the stage of legal proceedings and the specific questions faced by the legal decision maker impact the formulation of psycholegal questions. Finally, it reviews legal guidelines relevant to FMHA practice in child protection. The overall objective of this chapter is to convey forensic mental health concepts applicable to child protection evaluations. Procedures for implementing these concepts when conducting evaluations are covered in Chapters 4 through 7.

INFO

Whether a child protection evaluation is court-ordered or requested by a social service agency, it is likely to be used in court.

Clinical versus Forensic Assessment

The FMHA differs in several important ways from a clinical or therapeutic assessment. The following paragraphs summarize key differences between these assessment types, drawing generously from detailed discussions by Heilbrun et al. (2009) and Melton et al. (2007). Evaluations of parents in child protection may initially be conducted for treatment purposes but ultimately may be relied upon by courts, so it is necessary to consider the demands of FMHA from the outset. An evaluation takes on a "life of its own" once the report is written (Budd, 2001), and the evaluator cannot correct or update the report after the fact for use in court.

Scope

The purpose of FMHA is to assist the legal decision maker by identifying the examinee's functional capacity or impairment directly relevant to the legal issue. By contrast, the purpose of clinical or therapeutic assessment is to diagnose and treat symptoms. In a child protection context, the functional capacities of interest typically relate to the parent's ability to safely protect and care for a child. Issues of mental health diagnosis and treatment, which are prominent in clinical evaluations, are usually of less interest in the FMHA. However, because parent assessment often is used not only to guide courts but also to guide intervention or monitor progress, the scope of the assessment may be broadened beyond the typically narrower scope of the FMHA.

Importance of Client's Perspective

The client of a therapeutic assessment is usually the person being evaluated, whereas the "client" of the FMHA is the agency referring the parent and, ultimately, the court. Although it is important for the mental health professional (MHP) to strive to understand the parent's perspective, the parent's concerns or views are secondary to the primary focus of the FMHA, which is an objective assessment of the parent's functional capacities

INFO

Child protection evaluations typically focus on the parent's ability to protect and care for the child.

(American Psychological Association [APA], 1999: hereinafter referred to as APA, 1999). The FMHA seeks to provide information not already available to the court and to integrate information from multiple sources.

Voluntariness

Unlike therapeutic assessments, forensic assessments are generally compelled and should not be viewed as voluntary, even when the parent has readily agreed to the assessment. The parent would not be undergoing the assessment if not for the recommendation of the child protective services (CPS) agency or the court. Whether or not the assessment is formally ordered with specified consequences for not participating, the parent may justifiably anticipate a less favorable case outcome if the evaluation is refused. Thus, the element of voluntariness is absent (Baerger & Budd, 2003; Heilbrun, 2001). Consequently, the parent and parent's attorney may be provided Notification of Purpose (Connell, 2006; Heilbrun, 2001) in place of the Informed Consent that would occur in a therapeutic assessment. The limits of confidentiality should also be made clear (APA, 1999).

Autonomy

Similar to the absence of voluntariness, forensic assessment differs from therapeutic assessment in the degree of autonomy enjoyed by the examinee. The parent's autonomy is significantly curtailed by the compulsory nature of the evaluation and the power differential between the parent and CPS. The parent has little or no input regarding the goals of the assessment or techniques to be used.

Threats to Validity

The examinee in a therapeutic evaluation is generally motivated to be forthcoming and truthful to ensure an accurate and useful assessment. The FMHA examinee, however, has a significant stake in the outcome and may be motivated to deliberately distort self-reports to obtain the desired outcome. The parent may

INFO

Forensic assessments are not voluntary. Typically, child protection evaluations are ordered by the court or requested by a social service agency.

legitimately anticipate that adverse consequences could flow from the assessment, and is expected, accordingly, to be guarded and defensive about revealing unfavorable information.

Relationship and Dynamics

Therapeutic assessment often occurs within a "helping relationship" in which trust and understanding may have already been established. The FMHA evaluator maintains a more dispassionate, objective demeanor that serves as an appropriate reminder that the assessment is not being conducted for the purpose of helping the examinee. The MHP is respectful in interactions but maintains an air of impartiality and a certain emotional distance.

Pace and Setting

The FMHA differs from a therapeutic evaluation in that it occurs within a finite time and is not open-ended or ongoing. This necessitates careful planning and execution of the FMHA, often under conditions of limited resources and time constraints. It is important to gather the most complete and accurate information feasible, because omissions and errors in the report cannot be corrected after the legal decision is made.

Professional Guidelines for FMHA Practice in Child Protection

There are several general resources to guide the practitioner in performing FMHAs in child protection matters, including the APA Ethical Principles of Psychologists and Code of Conduct (2002); the Standards for Educational and Psychological Testing (American Educational Research Association, American Psychological Association, and National Council on Measurement in Education, 1999); the Specialty Guidelines for Forensic Psychologists (hereinafter referred to as the "Specialty Guidelines": Committee on Ethical Guidelines for Forensic Psychologists, 1991); and the American Psychological Association's Record Keeping Guidelines (2007). Of these, the Specialty Guidelines are particularly useful in clarifying how the legal context influences obligations of the MHP in forensic assessments. The Specialty

Guidelines call for objectivity with a careful consideration of alternative hypotheses to understand the data. They emphasize the unique limits on confidentiality and the importance of clarifying those limits to the examinee. They also call for a higher level of documentation than might be necessary in clinical settings, since the underlying data leading to the results of the evaluation must be accessible for review in the court.

The most relevant guidelines specifically for psychologists performing evaluations in child protection matters are the Guidelines for Psychological Evaluations in Child Protection Matters (APA, 1999). Some key recommendations in the guidelines include the importance of determining the scope of the evaluation based on the nature of the referral questions; informing participants about limits of confidentiality; using multiple methods of data gathering; making efforts to observe the child with the parent and recognizing the value of observation in natural settings; neither over-interpreting nor inappropriately interpreting assessment data; providing an opinion only after conducting an evaluation adequate to support conclusions; recognizing the need for timeliness; and gaining specialized competencies and knowledge (APA, 1999).

A particular referral issue in some child protection matters involves evaluation of suspected child sexual abuse. At the adjudication (pretrial) phase, forensic assessment may be requested as evidence in determining the credibility of sexual-abuse allegations. This topic, far too complex to be covered in the current volume on assessing parents in child protection matters, has stimulated a significant body of literature, including professional guidelines. These include Psychosocial Evaluation of Suspected Sexual Abuse in Children (American Professional Society on the Abuse of Children Task Force on the Psychosocial Evaluation of Suspected Sexual Abuse in Children, 1990; 1997; 2002); Use of

INFO

The Guidelines for Psychological Evaluations in Child Protection Matters are guidelines from the American Psychological Association to promote proficiency in using psychological expertise in conducting psychological evaluations in child protection matters.

INFO

A forensic assessment may be requested at the pretrial phase in cases of suspected child sexual abuse.

Anatomical Dolls in Child Sexual Abuse Assessments (American Professional Society on the Abuse of Children, 1995); and Policy Statement: Guidelines for the Clinical Evaluation for Child and Adolescent Sexual Abuse (American Academy of Child and Adolescent Psychiatry, 1990). The American Psychological Association has published a brief paper on the vicissitudes of memories of childhood abuse (1995) that may also be helpful to the MHP.

Frameworks for Formulating and Answering Questions in FMHAs

The first task for the FMHA is to identify the relevant forensic issues. There is an important difference between the legal question, which is the ultimate matter to be decided by the court, and the relevant forensic questions, which concern the parent's capacities and deficits that relate to the ultimate legal question (Grisso, 1986, 2003; Heilbrun et al., 2009). This section focuses on approaches to addressing the forensic questions. A discussion of the "ultimate issue" debate, which is related to the interpretation of assessment findings, is taken up in Chapter 6.

Identifying the relevant forensic issues begins with clarifying specific referral questions and ensuring that there are tools available to the FMHA to address the questions. What are the forensic questions, and how can they be operationalized so that their component parts become clear—and a determination can be made whether science lends itself to answering the questions (Otto & Edens, 2003)? The referral questions may require clarification; they may be vague (e.g., "to do a psychological evaluation"), overly broad (e.g., "to assess the parent's and child's needs and functioning"), or patently inappropriate by asking about the occurrence of a past event that is beyond the capacity of the MHP to discover ("to determine whether the parent abused the child"). There is an important distinction between the clinician's being asked whether a child has been abused and the clinician's being asked if the child has been harmed by known or acknowledged abuse (Melton et al., 2007). The former question is for the court to decide and is addressed at the adjudication phase. As noted earlier, a request for an FMHA relating to this question is most likely to arise in sexual abuse cases. MHPs should avoid reconsidering the evidence regarding whether or not abuse occurred unless specifically court-ordered to do so. By contrast, the latter question, regarding whether a child was harmed by abuse, is an appropriate topic for the FMHA across the life of a case. Through initial discussions with the referral source, the questions can be clarified and focused so that reasonable expectations and goals are established (Budd, 2001).

Certain limits are generally accepted in formulating opinions for the court. The evaluator guards against offering personal opinions on the legal matter and stays within the bounds of professional expertise. Opinions should flow from the data gathered and assimilated and should be firmly anchored in that data (APA, 2002; Heilbrun, 2001; Heilbrun et al., 2009; Committee on Ethical Guidelines for Forensic Psychologists, 1991). The ultimate legal question that is before the court often involves not only issues that may be within the expertise of testifying experts but issues that are best left to the juror or fact-finder—the value-laden or moral questions with which the law must grapple (Grisso, 2003; Heilbrun, 2001; Heilbrun et al., 2009). Expert testimony must be reliable and relevant (Sales & Shuman, 1998); therefore, the evaluator should offer an opinion only in the areas that fall within the evaluator's *professional* expertise.

This volume represents the current practices that are generally accepted as sound for evaluating parents in child protection matters. Although in some urban areas there may be model programs sufficiently funded to allow for extraordinarily comprehensive evaluations, the vast majority of evaluators work under more onerous conditions, a

BEWARE It is not your role to determine whether or not a child has been abused unless you are ordered by the court to do so. However, you may address the question of whether a child was harmed by abuse.

consideration reflected in the chapters guiding data collection and reporting. The lives of the parents and children who are the focus of evaluations in child protection matters are directly affected in far-reaching ways by the outcomes of their court cases, outcomes that often rely on the results of these assessments (Budd et al., 2004). This volume and the others that are part of the series (Heilbrun et al., 2009) were conceived to guide evaluators in identifying "best practice," as empirically supported, legally relevant, and consistent with applicable professional standards.

Several models have been proposed for applying psychological or psychiatric assessment processes to the needs of the legal system in evaluations of parenting (e.g., Azar, Lauretti, & Loding, 1998; Barnum, 1997; Budd, 2001, 2005; Condie, 2003; Dyer, 1999; Grisso, 1986, 2003; Kuehnle, Coulter, & Firestone, 2000; Pezzot-Pearce & Pearce, 2004; Reder & Lucey, 1995). Three approaches with broad relevance across forensic issues of parenting are described in the sections that follow.

Barnum's Four-H Model

Barnum (1997) outlined a comprehensive assessment method for cases of alleged child neglect and abuse and organized it around four assessment activities. They include (a) determining whether abuse occurred; (b) describing any harm to the child as a result of alleged or proven abuse or neglect; (c) describing the parent's caretaking capacities; and (d) offering a prognosis with recommendations for treatment and intervention. Barnum (2002) referred to these as the Four H's for organizing the inquiry and the data:

(1) What *happened*? The facts surrounding the allegations sometimes are in question, but, to the extent that the facts are known, the MHP may pay some heed to them as

INFO

There are several models for conducting child protection evaluations, including:

- Barnum's Four-H Model
- Grisso's Assessment of Competency Model
- Budd's Clinical Practice Model

background to an opinion regarding parenting capacity.

(2) What *harm* did it cause? Although it may be clear that the child was abused or neglected, the range of possible effects is substantial. Furthermore, alternative explanations for any apparent harm or symptoms of harm should be addressed. The physical harm a child may have suffered as a consequence of physical abuse or neglect is generally a medical matter. Developmental or emotional harm, on the other hand, may be a matter to be addressed by a MHP. It is often difficult to establish a clear nexus between the child's current functioning and any specific abuse or neglect. The assessment of the child's current functioning, of all known potential stressors or contributors, and carefully considered hypotheses about causation are of most use to the fact finder.

(3) What *help* can the parent provide? The focus of the assessment in Barnum's model is on formulating an opinion regarding the parent's current ability to provide adequate care to the child. Although the ultimate determination of adequacy is made by the fact finder, the MHP can address functional parenting capacity, a concept that may embrace a variety of different functions. Barnum recommended summarizing the salient findings and offering opinions on the nature and extent of particular strengths and weaknesses. Additionally, Barnum suggested that an opinion may be offered regarding whether the specific constellation of strengths and weaknesses would put this parent's child at risk of further abuse or neglect. This may be accompanied by a characterization of the level of risk and the specific precipitating factors that would tend to activate the risk.

(4) What *hope* is there for the future? Barnum's model includes the formulation of a prognosis and clinical recommendations to guide service planning and legal determinations. To the extent that any functional parenting deficits are linked to specific disorders for which treatment may be available, it is essential to note these and to offer a frank but appropriately cautious prognosis regarding realistic probabilities of improvement. Barnum suggested the MHP attend to (a) what is known empirically about the likely success of treatment interventions; (b) the parent's history of treatment, including successes and failures; (c) the parent's current recognition of the disorder and motivations for treatment; and (d) the parent's realistic access to adequate treatment, including availability, funding, transportation, and language and cultural matching. If the parent is not expected to be able to make good use of treatment, this should be noted and explained. When the nature of the deficit is not linked to a clinical disorder but rather is environmental, the MHP may offer suggestions about services that would be appropriate (Barnum, 2002, p. 93).

INFO

Barnum's Four-H Model of Assessment:

1. What happened?

2. What harm did it cause?

3. What help can the parent provide?

4. What hope is there for the future?

Grisso's Assessment of Competency Model

The court-bound or forensic assessment is guided by the specific legal question faced by the legal decision maker. This question frequently relates to determining an individual's cognitive or psychological (i.e., mental) competence (Grisso, 2003). In the context of child protection evaluations, the term *competence* usually refers to a parent's capacity to care for and protect the child (Budd, 2001). Another type of parental competence relevant to some child protection proceedings is a parent's competence to consent to various decisions about who will care for and parent the child (Baerger & Budd, 2003). Such questions may arise, for example, in voluntary relinquishment of parental rights or placing the child for adoption. In assessing a par-

ent's competence, the overarching consideration is the child's safety and well-being (APA, 1999).

Mental health data that may be relevant to the court in determining a parent's capabilities and how they relate to a child's best interests are virtually limitless. To operationalize parenting competency, it is helpful to examine functional, causal, interactive, judgmental, and dispositional elements (Baerger & Budd, 2003; Grisso, 2003).

FUNCTIONAL ELEMENTS
The evaluator asks, "What specific functional abilities must this parent possess in order to parent the specific child at a minimally adequate level?" This determination should center on what the parent understands, believes, knows, does, and is capable of doing related to caring for the child (Grisso, 1986, 2003). Functional assessment shifts the focus from diagnostic or trait-based qualities to direct measurement of parenting behaviors, capabilities, and practices (Budd, 2001).

CAUSAL ELEMENTS
The concept of legal competence, including parenting competence, requires causal inference to explain an individual's functional abilities or deficits (Grisso, 2003). Causal inference regarding a parent's expressed strong motivation to parent, for example, may include consideration that the parent is emotionally attached to the child or that the parent is dissimulating (Otto & Edens, 2003). A deficit in parenting ability may be caused by life-situational stressors, situational or examination-related stressors, ambivalence, lack

of information, or mental disorder or disability (Otto & Edens, 2003).

INTERACTIVE ELEMENTS

The parent's capacity for caregiving may depend on the interaction between the parent's functional ability and the degree of performance demanded by the specific circumstances (Grisso, 2003). An understanding of the child's needs is crucial to this determination, since children vary remarkably in terms of the ease with which they are parented. Parenting one child might be a manageable task for some parents, but parenting several young children might be overwhelmingly difficult. Adequate parenting might be possible under circumstances of low environmental stress, a good support system, and effective medication management, for instance, whereas the same parent, with the same child, might be incapacitated with sustained partner violence, poverty, absence of supportive resources, or inconsistent adherence to medication.

JUDGMENTAL AND DISPOSITIONAL ELEMENTS

When there is too great a discrepancy or incongruity between the parent's capacity and the situational demands, the judgment of incompetence may follow. Conversely, when the parent's capacity is more congruent with the demands, there may be a finding of competence (Grisso, 2003). The statute controlling termination of parental rights might include an allusion to this judgmental component with words such as "sufficient," "requisite," "unlikely to be able," and "within a reasonable length of time." The judgmental component is ultimately the fact finder's to determine, but the FMHA can be useful to that process by addressing, to the extent supported by the data, the elements with which the law must ultimately grapple. The fact finder has the responsibility to weigh the balance of interests between the risk of harm to a child and "a state's intrusion to sever a relationship recognized almost universally as having no equal for intimacy and privacy" (Otto & Edens, 2003, p. 256). It is determined on the basis of social and moral judgments, of "how much is enough," and it is beyond the specialized expertise of the MHP to make this determination (Grisso, 2003; Otto & Edens, 2003).

Budd's Clinical Practice Model

Budd (2001) proposed a model for evaluation of parents in child protection matters based on Grisso's (1986, 2003) general competence assessment model. Baerger and Budd (2003) extended the application of Grisso's model to the assessment of competence to consent to various decisions regarding who will care for and parent the child in cases of voluntary relinquishment of a child to adoption or guardianship. Budd's model of parenting capacity assessment contains three core features: a focus on parenting, functional parenting abilities, and a minimal parenting standard.

First, evaluation should include a focus on parental capabilities and deficits and on the parent–child relationship. Adult qualities and characteristics need to be linked to specific aspects of parental fitness or unfitness, by showing how they are a protective factor or a risk to the child or how they enable or prevent the parent from profiting from rehabilitative services. Thus, a focus on parenting qualities and the parent–child relationship is a core feature of Budd's model.

Second, a functional approach should be employed, emphasizing behaviors and skills in the everyday performance of parenting. Parenting skills should be assessed through examining the fit of parental skills and deficits with individual children's needs. Rather than concentrating on diagnostic and trait-based qualities, functional assessment focuses on direct measurement of parenting behaviors, capabilities, and practices. Functional assessment also embodies a constructive focus on identifying parenting strengths and areas of adequate performance, in contrast to a deficit-centered focus (Budd, 2001).

Third, the focus is on a minimal parenting standard. As Budd (2001, p. 3) argued: "Rather than comparing parents

INFO

The three core features of Budd's model of parenting capacity assessment are:

- A focus on parenting qualities and the parent–child relationship

- A functional approach emphasizing behaviors and skills in everyday performance

- Application of a minimal parenting standard

to adaptive or nurturing parents or comparing the relative abilities among caregivers (as in divorce custody cases), a lower standard is appropriate. Minimal parenting competency is the 'floor' of acceptable parenting that is sufficient to protect the safety and well being of the child." In the absence of an empirical or legal basis for imposing a more stringent criterion, the law protects parents' rights to raise their children as they choose. Research has found pervasive differences in parenting beliefs and practices associated with factors such as socioeconomic status, race, ethnicity, religion, and other human differences. As Budd (2001) stated:

> These factors do not exert direct effects on families resulting in "better" or "worse" parenting, but rather, research suggests that people of different groups have different experiences that make them different people, both in their beliefs and values and in their behaviors.... Adherence to a minimal parenting threshold fits with psychologists' ethical responsibilities to respect individual differences with regard to culture, access to resources, and community practices of childrearing. (p. 3)

The law has not adopted a universal model or standard to define minimally adequate parenting (Budd, 2001; Budd & Holdsworth, 1996; Melton et al., 2007). Lacking a definition in the law, forensic evaluators may turn to the fields of child development or child psychology to search for a universally accepted model. Research relating to the lower limits of parenting and the degree of parental competency sufficient for children to achieve developmental milestones is discussed in Chapter 3.

Comparison of Child Protection and Child Custody Evaluation Contexts

Questions of parental fitness arise not only in child protection cases but also in divorce proceedings. The increased use of mental health evaluators in divorce cases beginning in the 1970s coincided with greater attention to the "best interests" standard as a means for deciding custody based on characteristics of each child and parent (Otto & Edens, 2003). Coincidentally, the use of mental health evaluations in child protection evaluations focused initially on assessing parental fitness or unfitness in termination of parental rights cases and gradually expanded to dispositional decisions at earlier legal stages (e.g., regarding permanency goals, service needs, or visitation arrangements: Melton et al., 2007). Increasing reports of child maltreatment in the 1990s, particularly in large urban centers, precipitated requests for mental health evaluations of parents as dependency courts and child welfare agencies attempted to deal with the backlog of cases (Budd et al., 2001; Dyer, 1999).

There are important distinctions between the issues at stake in child protection and child custody cases, as shown in Table 2.1. A fundamental difference is that, in child-custody evaluations, both parents are presumed capable of providing at least minimally

2
chapter

Table 2.1 | Comparison of Child Custody and Child Protection Evaluations

Child Custody	Child Protection
Presumption of minimally adequate parenting	No presumption of minimally adequate parenting
Stakes involve distribution of parenting time and responsibility	Stakes involve conditions of access (e.g., visitation) and eventual reunification versus termination of rights
Focus on child's best interests	Focus on child's best interests and parent's rights
Animosity between parents likely	Animosity between parents and state likely
Varied Socio-Economic Status	Typically low SES
Broad focus of evaluation	Narrow focus of evaluation

adequate caregiving, and the evaluation is designed to ascertain custodial arrangements that are in the child's best interests. By contrast, child protection evaluations are designed to address the parent's ability to provide minimally adequate care. Whereas child custody evaluations inherently involve comparisons between the parents and their relationships with the child, child protection evaluations typically do not (and should not) involve comparing the parent or the parent–child relationship to that of a temporary caregiver (e.g., a foster parent).

The differing goals and circumstances of child custody and child protection courts limit the relevance of custody-related models and legal guidelines in parental assessments at issue in this volume.

Referral Questions at Various Stages of the Case

Referral questions differ across various stages of CPS involvement. Budd and Springman's (in press) analysis of referral questions in one large urban juvenile court system found that the most common referral issues concerned service planning, parenting ability, or the parent's cognitive or emotional functioning, whereas issues of the child's behavior or needs were less frequently addressed. Referrals from social service agencies often involved no pending legal decision; rather, the clinical information was requested primarily for service planning purposes. The most commonly cited pending legal decisions were selection or change of a permanency goal and visitation arrangements. Whether these patterns are typical of other court systems is unknown, but they demonstrate the variety of referral concerns present across cases.

Despite the diversity of potential forensic issues, some questions are more likely than others to arise during the lifetime of a child protection case. After CPS has established a basis for involvement with a family, the referral for FMHA may be driven by a need to refine casework goals and plans. Questions at this stage may be, for example, "What strengths and deficits does this parent have in providing adequate care for three toddlers?" or "What are this parent's service needs, given the parent's history of chronic depression?" or "What is the parent's mental health status, and how does it impact his or her ability to parent the child?" At this early stage of intervention, evaluation questions may address the parent's receptivity to substance-abuse intervention or the parent's capacity to understand the child's developmental level and limitations.

After working with a parent for a period of time, the CPS caseworker may identify previously unknown issues that form the basis for assessment or may want assistance in understanding a parent's failure to adhere to intervention recommendations. Sample questions include, "How does the pattern of partner violence in this parent's relationships interact with the capacity to parent and ability to cooperate with the service plan?" or "What is the prognosis for positive change with regard to the parent's chemical dependency?" Should interventions fail, the question may be, "What has interfered with the parent's cooperation with the recommended psychiatric treatment regimen, and can these obstacles be resolved in a reasonable timeframe?" or "What are realistic expectations about whether the parent can adhere to necessary medication schedules in order to meet functional parenting demands for the two-year-old child?" There also may be concerns about the safety of the visitation arrangements or the impact of extended out-of-home care on the parent–child relationship.

Later stages of the case may give rise to referral concerns relating to planning for reunification or, in the absence of progress, termination of parental rights, permanent guardianship, or adoption. When considering termination of parental rights, the referral questions are likely to focus on whether the parent's functioning meets statutory criteria for "unfitness" as defined in state law. Questions also may relate to whether the parent's current condition impacts the ability to discharge parental responsibilities, and, if so, whether this condition will extend beyond a reasonable time period. At voluntary relinquishment of parental rights, the evaluation questions may focus on the parent's understanding of the implications of the relinquishment.

At any stage, questions may focus on what is in the best interests of the child. For example, "What would be the implications for the child of returning to live with his mother after 18 months in the foster home?" or "How has the child adjusted to unsupervised day visits with the father, and what are the risk and protective factors for the child of extending visitation from unsupervised daytime to overnight visits?" Differing methods of assessment may be required, depending on the referral questions. Chapter 4 describes strategies for formulating specific referral questions in relation to the issues before the court.

Legal Guidelines for FHMA Practice in Child Protection

Statutes and case law explicate how trial judges determine, upon challenge, whether to allow expert testimony on an issue. Generally, expert testimony, scientific or otherwise, must be both relevant and reliable to be admissible (*Daubert v. Merrell Dow Pharmaceuticals*, 1995; *Frye v. United States*, 1923; *Kuhmo Tire v. Carmichael*, 1999; and state equivalents). In addition to general threshold criteria for opinion testimony to be both based on reliable methodology and relevant, there may be specific case law regarding the admissibility of ultimate-issue testimony in cases dealing with allegations of child abuse. The law has clearly established that testimony framed in terms of the child's truthfulness ("I believed the child's report of sexual abuse because...") is not permissible, particularly from experts, whose opinions may be given more weight than those of lay witnesses. The judge or jury must make the determination of truthfulness (Melton et al., 2007). Although experts may be asked to form such opinions and to offer them in reports and in testimony, it is not proper to do so. Chapter 7 provides further discussion of the issues in offering expert testimony.

BEWARE
In cases of alleged child abuse, expert testimony framed in terms of the child's truthfulness is not permissible. It is up to the trier of fact, not the expert witness, to determine truthfulness.

In the absence of a uniform definition of minimally adequate parenting, one way of operationalizing the concept might be to examine component elements sometimes arising in the law. It is at the point of termination of parental rights (TPR) on the claim that the parent has failed to maintain minimally adequate parenting that some case law fleshes out the elements. First, an examination of parental disability and its interaction with minimally adequate parenting is in order. Second, the general concept of parental unfitness will be examined.

Disability and Termination of Parental Rights

When parents are physically or mentally disabled to such an extent that their parenting capacities are limited, the law provides direction. First, antidiscrimination statutes and laws bear consideration in understanding how a disabling condition should be viewed in the face of child maltreatment. Second, in spite of these protections, many state statutes identify disability as a basis for consideration for termination. Third, the reconciliation of these disparate forces may be in a careful functional assessment of the disabling condition, the accommodations or interventions that are needed to bridge the gap to minimally adequate parenting, and the parent's capacity to use such an accommodation or intervention.

Despite the passage in 1990 of the Americans with Disabilities (ADA) Act (U.S. Equal Opportunity Employment Commission, 1990), intended to protect persons with disabilities from discrimination, state TPR statutes may still be frankly discriminatory. A review of all state statutes revealed in 2007 that 36 states and the District of Columbia include disability as a basis for discrimination, while 15 states do not (Center for Advanced Studies in Child Welfare, University of Minnesota, n.d.). Those that include "disability" specify the types of disability—all 36 states specify mental illness; 32 states include intellectual or developmental disability; 18 states include emotional illness; and 7 states include physical disability. The language describing the disability may be vague or imprecise; for example, 11 states include the language, "emotional illness, mental illness and mental deficiency." Some specific examples of codified language addressing disability illustrate the general nature of these statutes.

Illinois's code notes that expedited procedures for termination may be mobilized when a ground for unfitness is met and the parent is unable to discharge his or her parental duties due to mental illness, mental deficiency, or developmental disability (Ill. Comp. Stat. Ch. 705, § 405/1-2; Ch 750, § 50/1). Similarly, an Ohio statute provides that a court may terminate parental rights if it finds, by clear and convincing evidence, that it is in the best interests of the child and that, among other circumstances, the parent is unable to discharge his or her parental duties due to chronic mental or emotional illness, mental retardation, or physical disability (Ohio Rev. Code Ann. § 2151.414).

A Kansas statute provides that the court may terminate parental rights when it finds, by clear and convincing evidence, that the parent is unfit by reason of conduct or condition that renders the parent unable to care properly for a child, and the conduct or condition is unlikely to change in the foreseeable future. Among conditions to be considered are "[e]motional illness, mental illness, mental deficiency, or physical disability of such duration or nature as to render the parent unable to care for the child" (Kan. Ann. Stat. §§ 38-2269; 38-2271). California's statute lists circumstances that are grounds for termination of parental rights without the necessity for provision of reunification services beforehand, including "clear and convincing evidence... that the parent is suffering from a mental disability that renders him or her incapable of utilizing reunification services" (Cal. Welf. & Inst. Code §§ 361.5; 366.26). Idaho, by contrast, changed the state code in 2005 to comport with ADA protections. It noted that, when the state considers possible termination of parental rights against a parent with a disability, "... the parent shall have a right to provide evidence to the court regarding the manner in which adaptive equipment or supportive services will enable the parent to carry out parenting responsibilities" (Idaho Code § 16-2005).

Given that statutory grounds for TPR in many states include the parent's long-term mental illness or deficiency (and in some states also the parent's long-term alcohol- or drug-induced incapacity: Child Welfare Information Gateway, 2007), the referral for forensic evaluation may be specifically focused on determining whether the condition exists. The MHP should be explicit in identifying functional implications of a parental disability and possible adaptive equipment or supportive services that would allow the individual to parent in a minimally adequate fashion. Further, the MHP should seek out data that bears on the individual's willingness to accept such adaptations or services. The mere presence of the disability, while potentially statutorily sufficient for termination in states that retain discriminatory or vague language, does not necessarily lead to an ethically justifiable conclusion that a parent is unfit. Regardless of the specificity of the state statute addressing disability, the relevance of the disability to functional parenting capacities must be addressed. When the disability does not appear to constrain adequate parenting, this should be clearly stated. These conditions should (and in some statutes, do) form the basis for termination *only* if they demonstrably interfere with parenting. Thus the FMHA must both investigate the presence of the impairment and also amass behavioral data establishing a nexus between the long-term impairment and the consequent incapacity to parent.

INFO

Some states identify disability (either physical or mental) as grounds for termination of parental rights. As a result, child protection evaluations in these cases should focus on identifying the disability and how it affects parenting capacity and on determining what accommodations can be made to allow the parent to meet minimal parenting requirements.

Unfitness and Termination of Parental Rights

The legal context in which a parental fitness evaluation arises may be couched within the statute addressing termination of parental rights, the ultimate legal outcome when there is no other way to ensure the child's protection. All jurisdictions have statutes providing for the legal termination of parental rights (Child Welfare Information Gateway, 2007). Termination, which may be voluntary or involuntary, ends the legal parent–child relationship. The child becomes a ward of the state and is legally freed for adoption. When the termination is sought by the state and is involuntary, the court must determine by clear and convincing evidence

(*Santosky v. Kramer,* 1982) that termination of parental rights is in the child's best interests.

FMHAs conducted at the termination phase of a case, or offered in evidence at that phase, invoke heightened concerns for forensic mental health professionals. The gravity of the consequences to children and their parents cannot be overstated. Rarely do either parents or children have access to aggressive legal protections. These cases may be viewed, even at the courthouse, as social-work problems rather than as legal contests wherein each side has legitimate interests that deserve fair judicial consideration.

INFO

Common grounds for termination of parental rights include:

● Severe or chronic abuse or neglect

● Abuse or neglect of other children in the household

● Abandonment

● Long-term mental illness or deficiency of the parent(s)

● Long-term alcohol- or drug-induced incapacity of the parents(s)

● Failure to support or maintain contact with the child

● The involuntary termination of the rights of the parent to another child

● Felony conviction of the parent(s) for a crime of violence against the child or another family member, or a conviction for any felony when the term of incarceration is so long as to have a negative impact on the child, and the only available provision of care for the child is foster care (Child Welfare Information Gateway, 2007, p. 1).

Melton et al. (2007) noted that the combined problems of vague standards for minimally adequate parenting and the propensity for recommendations to derive from individual value judgments become magnified at the termination phase in child abuse and neglect cases. When parental unfitness is not clearly and objectively defined but rather is case fact–driven, criteria may be applied arbitrarily from case to case. Mental illness, mental retardation, morally questionable behavior, or chemical dependency may justify consideration for termination in one case or jurisdiction but not in another. MHPs can contribute to an increased fairness of the proceedings by offering clear, objective information about the functional implications of whatever parental characteristics have prevented adequate parenting. The FMHA also can help by specifying what services might have been effective at ameliorating the deficits, how the parent responded to available services, what prevented positive change, and what future parental functioning may reasonably be expected, given the history of the parent's response to intervention.

State statutes for termination of parental rights vary but may include many grounds in common.

As discussed in Chapter 1, the Adoption and Safe Families Act (ASFA, 1997) requires the states to provide reasonable efforts to prevent out-of-home placement or to achieve reunification of the family after placement has failed to correct the conditions that led to removal. Whether the state has provided reasonable efforts may become the focal point of the legal dispute, and the FMHA may be one opportunity for objective assessment of the parent's utilization of services and of the barriers that may have inhibited maximal use of intervention (Youth Law Center, 2000). About 20 states and the District of Columbia require the petition for termination to confirm that the state included these reunification efforts in a service plan (Child Welfare Information Gateway, 2007). Specifically, ASFA (1997) required petitions for termination under the following conditions: (1) The child has been in foster care for 15 of the most recent 22 months; and (2) a court has determined (a) the child to be an abandoned infant; or (b) the parent has committed murder or voluntary manslaughter of another child of the parent; has aided and abetted, attempted, conspired, or solicited to commit such a murder or voluntary manslaughter; or has committed a felony assault that has resulted in serious bodily injury to the child or another child of the parent. In enacting ASFA, Congress recognized there are cases in which TPR is inappropriate or impractical, and it provided the following three exceptions to the requirement to initiate termination of parental rights proceedings (ASFA, §302(4), 42 U.S.C. §675(5)(E)):

(1) The child is being cared for by a relative (if the state elects to include this exception);

(2) A state agency has documented in the case plan (which shall be available for court review) a compelling reason for determining that filing such a petition would not be in the best interests of the child; or

(3) The state determines that certain services identified in the child's case plan are necessary for the child's safe return home, but it has failed to provide them according to the schedule specified in the case plan.

However, states vary in how they interpret the *"compelling reason" clause*. The Center for the Study of Social Policy (2005) undertook a study to explore how states and jurisdictions were operationalizing this clause. A review of state statutes revealed that, as of 2003, no state had comprehensively defined in law the "compelling reasons" why termination of parental rights would not be in the child's best interests. Some states, including Iowa, West Virginia, and Oregon, provide examples in their state law. Iowa's law defines "a compelling reason" to include, but not be limited to, documentation of reasonable likelihood that completion of services will make it possible for the child to safely remain home or return home within six months (Iowa Code § 232.111). In West Virginia (W VA Code § 49-6-5b), New York (NY CLS Soc Serv § 384-b), and California (Cal. Wel. & Inst Code § 366.26), compelling reasons include the child's age and preference regarding termination of parental rights. California also provides an exception when the parent has maintained contact with the child and the child would benefit from continuing the relationship.

The Center for the Study of Social Policy (2005) developed the following criteria that might be considered compelling reasons for CPS not to file a TPR petition. Note that these suggested criteria have no applicability unless they have been codified in a jurisdiction; however, they do reflect a comprehensive analysis of the kinds of issues that might argue for not filing. They also provide MHPs with some context, in the absence of specific statutory criteria in the relevant jurisdiction, for potentially relevant foci for the FMHA when termination of parental rights is being considered.

(1) There is a permanency goal of returning home approved by the court, with the expectation that the child will be reunited with parents within six months. The caseworker must document evidence in the case record that the parent is making substantial progress in eliminating problems causing the child's placement in foster care or subsequent problems that contributed to the child's continued foster care.

(2) The child is a specified age (suggested age is 14) or older and objects to being adopted. The caseworker must document evidence in the case record that the child has participated in specific counseling to discuss all permanency options and understands all the permanency options.

(3) The child has severe emotional or behavioral problems or a serious medical condition, and reunification remains an appropriate goal. This reason needs to be documented in the case record with supported clinical evidence of the child's severe emotional, behavioral, or medical issues and the need for placement in residential treatment or other intensive treatment. The record should provide evidence that the parent is actively involved in the child's life and is planning for the child's return home.

(4) The child has a permanency goal other than adoption (i.e., permanency with kin through guardianship) and is expected to achieve that goal within 12 months of establishing the goal.

(5) Parents are deceased or have voluntarily relinquished rights or consented to adoption by a relative or identified caregiver, or have indicated they will do so within 30 days. If relinquishment or consent does not occur within specified time frame, the compelling-reasons determination should be eliminated.

(6) A petition for adoption has been filed with the court.

(7) The parent is terminally ill, does not want parental rights terminated, and has designated the child's present caretaker, with the caretaker's agreement, as the child's permanent caretaker. For children with a parent in prison and an expected release date within a short, specified period of time (e.g., six months), this reason might be used once in each case.

(8) The child is an unaccompanied refugee minor as defined in 45 Code of Federal Regulations 400.11.

(9) There are no, or insufficient, legal grounds for filing a TPR because required reasonable efforts have not been made. This determination could not be made without legal and supervisory review and documentation of the finding in the case record. In addition, this finding should require a case plan revision with specific actions to make reasonable efforts and frequent (every three to six months) review of progress.

(10) There are international legal obligations or compelling foreign policy reasons that would preclude terminating parental rights. (pp. 7-8).

Legal statutes regarding parental unfitness as it relates to termination of parental rights may provide some peripheral boundaries for the concept of minimally adequate parenting (Budd, 2005). On the whole, however, a professional consensus appears to have emerged (see, e.g., Azar et al., 1995; Budd, 2001; Budd & Holdsworth, 1996; and Jacobsen, Miller, & Kirkwood, 1997) that the MHP's focus should remain on a "minimal" standard rather than on some higher criterion for which no empirical or legal basis has been established (Budd, 2005). The evaluator is encouraged to bear in mind that cultural, ethnic, and economic differences in parenting standards exist and that it is unreasonable to expect everyone to achieve or maintain a "best parenting practices" level (APA, 1999). Retaining a behaviorally descriptive approach that is sensitive to these differences leaves room for the legal decision maker to determine the societal standard to which parents should be held. Minimally adequate parenting standards are not explicit and may be decided on a case-by-case basis.

The termination of parental rights is the last resort, then, when there are no alternatives to ensure the protection and well being of a child. It is a matter so grave that the MHP must understand the statutory context in which the case will be considered but also carefully attend to professional ethical obligations to limit recommendations to those clearly supported by the data. There is little place for speculation or personal emotional reactions in the evaluation process.

2
chapter

Summary

There is a delicate balance between the law's regard for the sanctity of the parent–child relationship and its responsibility to act responsibly to protect children who are maltreated. When there is reason to suspect that a child is in danger, there is a need for evidence to assist the court in determining parenting capacity, a need for which the courts may turn to behavioral scientists. Mental health providers contribute to the court's understanding of the risks the child may be facing, the services that might ameliorate the risk, and the potential for positive change.

The evaluation of parental fitness in child protection matters is distinct from a clinical evaluation in several important respects. Although the evaluation may be used to inform treatment or casework planning, it may eventually be introduced in court and may have far-reaching legal implications affecting the lives of the parent and child. Clinical observations or opinions may lack the requisite reliability for such extraordinary consequences. The evaluator can provide important information for clinical and casework planning and remain on defensible ground, not overstepping the data, by observing the distinction between recommended interventions and prognostication. Legal grounds for termination of parental rights sometimes identify potentially disabling conditions; however, these conditions do not always preclude minimally adequate parenting. An important evaluative task is to examine the nexus between the parent's abilities and limitations and the child's needs and capacities. Cultural and contextual issues should be fairly and fully explored in a respectful evaluative atmosphere with an eye to law's need to balance the parent's and child's rights. Evaluators need to understand the important differences between evaluations conducted in a child protection context from those conducted in a child custody context and apply a minimal parenting threshold in weighing the evidence on parenting strengths and weaknesses.

Empirical Foundations and Limits | **3**

Parenting, child development, and child maltreatment are enormously popular topics among social scientists. A comprehensive review of these literatures is far beyond the scope of this volume. Instead, this chapter provides a selective overview of behavioral and social science research as a backdrop to forensic mental health assessment of parents. It also reviews the limited research literature on forensic assessment relevant to parenting capacity evaluations. Four broad areas are covered: (1) descriptive research on parents and children involved in child protection cases and the services they have received; (2) conceptual frameworks and supporting research on parenting related to child maltreatment; (3) research on measures used in forensic evaluations of parents; and (4) research on forensic assessment practice—i.e., studies on how examiners collect information and how courts use this information. As Melton and colleagues (2007) concluded in their review of the child abuse and neglect literature, the scientific foundation is weak for predictions of child maltreatment and for the efficacy of interventions. Furthermore, they noted that methods of assessing parenting and family relationships in child protection have not, for the most part, been formally validated. The research described in this chapter is largely consistent with these conclusions; however, advances in a few areas suggest promising directions for development.

Parents and Children Involved in Child Protection Proceedings

For parents and children to become parties in child protection proceedings, there must be a substantiated report of child abuse or neglect, and a state must file a legal petition asking the court to determine the child's safety and need for placement. What characterizes families formally involved in the child protection system, what services do parents and children receive, and what are the outcomes? Answers to these questions provide a context for understanding the population and issues involved in FMHAs in child protection.

Incidence

Although little research exists on the subset of parents referred for FMHAs, general descriptions are available on the incidence and characteristics of parents and children known or alleged to have been involved in maltreatment. A major caveat, however, is that estimates of child maltreatment vary widely depending on the definitions and methods used (Feerick et al., 2006; Miller-Perrin & Perrin, 2007). The most comprehensive, conservative, and widely used database on incidence of child maltreatment comes from cases reported to child protection agencies. The National Child Abuse and Neglect Data System (NCANDS) is a federally mandated reporting system for tracking cases of child maltreatment (U.S. Department of Health and Human Services [DHHS], 2009). NCANDS publishes annual reports of national- and state-level findings of maltreated children and their perpetrators. In 2007, an estimated 3.2 million referrals were made on approximately 5.8 million children reported for investigation. Only 62% of the allegations were investigated; the remainder was screened out, mainly for insufficient information. Twenty-five percent of the cases investigated found at least one child to be a victim of abuse or neglect. This amounts to approximately 794,000 child victims annually. As in prior years, neglect was the most common form of maltreatment, reported in over one half (59%) of cases. Eleven percent of victims suffered physical abuse, 8% sexual abuse, and

4% emotional abuse (the balance of children experienced other or multiple forms of maltreatment). The youngest children had the highest rates of victimization, with proportionally lower rates as children aged. An estimated 1,760 fatalities were attributed to child abuse and neglect, and over three-quarters (76%) of the children killed were under four years of age.

The NCANDS database indicates that parents were the most frequent perpetrators of child maltreatment, accounting for 80% of all cases. Compared to fathers, mothers more often were perpetrators, probably because mothers traditionally have the major responsibility for childcare. For victims of sexual abuse, however, the percentage of parent perpetrators was far lower than for other types of maltreatment: 27% were abused by a parent, 29% by a relative other than a parent, 9% by an unmarried partner of the parent, and the remainder by another person. Nearly 9 out of 10 sexual abuse perpetrators, regardless of their relationship to the victim, were male (Sedlak & Broadhurst, 1996). Girls were sexually abused about three times more often than boys, whereas gender differences were small for victims of other types of maltreatment.

3 chapter

Racial and Ethnic Disparities

Patterns of maltreatment by racial and ethnic groups are complicated to unravel and have shown disparate findings across databases (Sedlak & Broadhurst, 1996). NCANDS rates of maltreatment for African American children are almost twice as high as those for Hispanic and White children. Other groups (e.g., American Indian or Alaskan Native, Mixed Race, and Pacific Islander) are lower than African Americans but higher than Hispanic and White groups, and Asian Americans are much lower than all others. Racial and ethnic disparities also have been documented in the number and types of child welfare services provided to families following substantiated abuse or neglect, time spent in care, and outcomes, with less favorable findings for children of color (Courtney et al., 1996).

In light of concerns about overrepresentation of some minorities in child protection, Congress commissioned a comprehensive study by the U.S. Government Accounting Office (GAO) (2007). The primary questions were directed at understanding the overrepresentation of African Americans in foster care and strategies to address this issue. The GAO found that while African American children make up only 15% of the national child population, they represent 34% of the foster care population. American Indians represent 1% of the general population and 2% of the foster care population, and a multi-ethnic constituency identified as "Other" by the GAO represents only 2% of the child population, while representing 5% of the foster care population. By contrast, White children make up 59% of the population and 41% of the foster care population.

Once removed from their homes, African American children are less likely than other children to be reunited with their families or adopted (GAO, 2007). Further, the GAO identified several factors contributing to a disproportionate number of African American children entering and remaining in foster care. These include higher rates of poverty, challenges in accessing support services, racial bias or cultural misunderstandings between child welfare decision makers and the families they serve, and difficulties finding permanent homes. The GAO recommended strategies for addressing some of the disparities based on promising practices reported by some of the states they studied.

The research on racial and ethnic disparities in the child protection system is relevant to parenting -capacity assessment for several reasons. First, ethnic minorities comprise a relatively large proportion of parents referred for evaluation, contrasted with the majority-ethnic background of most mental health professionals. Thus, training in ethnic diversity issues, cultural sensitivity, and awareness of the impact of one's own cultural identity is integral to developing evaluative competency (American Psychological Association Committee on Professional Practice and Standards [APA], 1999; Azar & Goff, 2007). Second, the factors shown to contribute to more minorities entering and remaining in foster care (e.g., poverty, lack of access to services, and biases in service provision) need to be considered as contextual factors when conducting forensic evaluations. These issues will be covered in more detail in Chapters 4 through 7, which deal with preparing for and conducting forensic evaluations and interpreting and reporting findings.

Factors Associated with Increased Risk

The NCANDS data provide a thumbnail sketch of the victims and perpetrators of maltreatment, but this sketch reveals little about the patterns and characteristics associated with its occurrence. Early etiological studies based on clinical descriptions of known abusers pointed to psychological characteristics of adults, such as personality problems and low intelligence, as predictors (Kempe et al., 1962; Steele & Pollock, 1968). Descriptive reports of cases in child protection proceedings based on selected court samples (e.g., Bishop et al., 2003; Llewellyn, McConnell, & Ferronato, 2003; Taylor et al., 1991) have confirmed an over-representation of parents with psychiatric, intellectual, or substance-abuse problems compared to the general population. However, research suggests that only a small proportion of perpetrators have severe personality or cognitive impairments. Rather, studies have expanded the list of potential antecedents to cover multiple parental characteristics as well as child, family, and environmental factors.

Commonly cited parent factors include individual characteristics (e.g., anger-control difficulties, low self-esteem, mental health problems, alcohol or drug abuse, physical health problems, cognitive impairments, and a history of having been abused as a child) and parenting patterns (e.g., unrealistic expectations, harshness, or rigidity). Child factors include young age, behavioral difficulties, and mental and physical disabilities. Family and environmental factors include single-parent status, low socioeconomic status (SES), unemployment, partner conflict, social isolation, community violence, and sparse resources (cf. Krug et al., 2002; Miller-Perrin & Perrin, 2007; Myers et al., 2002). Considerable overlap exists among risk factors for different types of maltreatment, although some characteristics are more frequently associated with a particular type of maltreatment (e.g., low SES with neglect; male perpetrator with sexual abuse) than others. Importantly, etiological studies have demonstrated that none of these characteristics is determinative of maltreatment, although as the number of risk factors increases, the likelihood of abuse or neglect increases (Brown et al., 1998).

The most tragic consequence of abuse or neglect is child death, and, unfortunately, it is difficult to predict which events will be fatal. The majority of child victims and their perpetrators had no prior contact with CPS at the time of the death (National Maternal and Child Health Center for Child Death Review, 2008). According to the 2007 NCANDS statistics, children whose families had received family preservation services in the past five years accounted for just 12% of child fatalities, and 3% of the child fatalities had been in foster care and were reunited with their families in the past five years (U.S. DHHS, 2009). A post-hoc study examining 26 fathers who murdered their children found an overrepresentation of stepfathers, a strong history of prior violence toward both the child and the child's mother, and young victims (all under age 4: Cavanaugh, Dobash, & Dobash, 2007), suggesting potential risk factors for child homicide. Risk factors identified for child death are listed in Table 3.1.

Functioning, Services Received, and Efficacy of Interventions

A major responsibility of the child protection system, in addition to investigating reports of maltreatment, is to provide services to maximize children's safety, promote permanent living arrangements, and facilitate children's development (Haskins, Wulczyn, & Webb, 2007). Kerker and Dore (2006) found estimates of children with emotional and behavioral maladjustment in community samples ranging from 16% to 22%. By comparison, for children in foster care, they found estimates ranging up to 80%. It is widely

Table 3.1 | Major Risk Factors for Child Death (National Maternal and Child Health Center for Child Death Review, 2008)

- Younger children, especially under the age of five.

- Parents or caregivers who are under the age of 30.

- Low-income, single-parent families experiencing major stresses.

- Children left with male caregivers who lack emotional attachment to the child.

- Children with emotional and health problems.

- Lack of suitable childcare.

- Substance abuse by caregivers.

- Parents and caregivers with unrealistic expectations of child development.

acknowledged that the states often fall short in meeting the complex needs of children in foster care (Annie M. Casey Foundation, 2009). Problems have included inadequate training and frequent turnover of child welfare staff, a shortage of high-quality foster homes, a dearth of effective intervention services, systemic resistance to implementing promising practices, resource limitations, and ineffective systems of accountability (Kauffman Best Practices Project, 2004).

In an effort to inform policy and practice, Congress commissioned the National Survey of Child and Adolescent Well-Being (NSCAW) as part of the 1996 federal welfare reform legislation (Haskins et al., 2007). The survey's purpose was to follow a representative national sample of children reported to child protective services to identify their functioning, the types of services they and their parents received, and their developmental outcomes.

Data were collected on over 5,000 children and their parents using multiple sources and measures over a three-year period beginning in 2000.

Highlights of some of the survey findings are listed in Table 3.2. Overall, the survey results revealed that children and parents who have contact with the child protection system have high rates of problems, complicated service needs, and frustratingly low levels of successful outcomes. Among the most disconcerting findings was that fewer than one-third of the children in out-of-home placement were returned home after 18 months in foster care, and only slightly more returned home by 36 months after placement. Sadly, one-quarter of the reunifications were unsuccessful, requiring the children to reenter the child protection system. These findings illustrate the challenges courts and child welfare agencies face in achieving the goals of child protection. The findings provide a context for understanding why FMHAs may be requested on parents during child protection proceedings.

A small body of research has examined the effectiveness of interventions in child maltreatment. Unfortunately, the data are limited and the evidence largely disappointing, particularly when measured in terms of behavioral change (e.g., Chaffin & Friedrich, 2004; Kauffman Best Practices Project, 2004). A meta-analysis of treatment outcome studies from 1974 to 2000 (Skowron & Reinemann, 2005) found moderately positive treatment effects, although the strength of the findings varied with the type of outcome measured. Treatment effects were weakest when measured by objective behavioral observations of the family and strongest when measured by parental self-report. Likewise, the evidence base for the effectiveness of programs to prevent child maltreatment is relatively weak (Reynolds, Mathieson, & Topitzes, 2008).

Despite ample evidence of serious shortcomings in the child welfare system, an important contribution of the research is that it provides comprehensive information that could enable researchers, policymakers, and practitioners to improve existing practices. The report of the Surgeon General's Conference on Children's Mental Health (Office of the Surgeon General, 2000) focused attention on the chronic, unmet mental health problems of

Table 3.2 | Selective Findings of the National Survey of Child and Adolescent Well-Being (reported in Haskins, Wulczyn, & Webb, 2007)

Topic	Findings
Child Problems	47% of children aged three years and younger with confirmed abuse and neglect had developmental delays upon entering the system, but fewer than one-fourth of these children were identified by their caseworkers as having problems (Rosenberg, Smith, & Levinson, 2007)
	48% of children aged 2–14 years at the time of investigation had clinically significant emotional and/or behavior problems (Burns et al., 2004)
Family Problems	45% of female caregivers involved in child welfare had experienced intimate-partner violence in their lifetimes, and 29% had experienced violence in the year preceding involvement in the child welfare system (Hazen et al., 2007)
	Children with clinically significant disruptive or aggressive behavior problems upon entering the system were 3.4 times more likely to have a parent with alcohol, drug, or mental health problems and 3.4 times more likely to have a parent with impaired parenting skills (Libby et al., 2007)
Services	Children with clinically elevated emotional and/or behavior problems were much more likely to receive mental health services than low-scoring youth, but only one-fourth received any specialty mental health care during the first 12 months of their involvement in the child welfare system (Burns et al., 2004)
	Parent-training programs frequently were included as part of the case plan for families; however, very few programs employed evidence-based models shown in research to be effective in changing parent behavior (Hurlburt et al., 2007)
Outcomes	By 18 months after out-of-home placement, 30% of children aged 0–14 years had returned home to their parents. Differing patterns of variables were associated with reunification across age groups. When controlling for other factors, parental compliance with the case plan was strongly related to reunification for children aged 0–5 years, whereas at least weekly visitation with their mothers was related to reunification for children older than 10 years (Wildfire, Barth, & Green, 2007).
	Children placed in out-of-home care following child protective investigation had an average of 2.9 placements in the first 18 months (range of 1–13 placements). By 36 months after placement, 34% returned home, but one-quarter of the reunifications were unsuccessful, so these children eventually returned to foster care (Rubin, O'Reilly, Hafner, Luan, & Localio, 2007).

children and adolescents. In response, policymakers advocated increased services, and researchers teamed with practitioners to develop evidence-based practices (EBPs). The result has been a growing number of programs with demonstrated success in treating a range of children's mental health problems (Eyberg, Nelson, & Boggs, 2008; Weisz, Jensen-Doss, & Hawley, 2006). Much like the Surgeon General's report catalyzed action on behalf of children's mental health, the NSCAW and other studies promise to spur support for EBPs with children and families in the child protection system. One example of such increased attention is the California Evidence-Based Clearinghouse for Child Welfare (CEBC) website (http://www.cachildwelfareclearinghouse.org/). CEBC was established in 2006 to identify and disseminate information regarding promising programs relevant to child welfare.

Researchers have analyzed program outcomes directly relevant to the child welfare system (e.g., rates of child abuse and neglect, out-of-home placement, and permanency) and the cost-effectiveness these programs (Lee, Aos, & Miller, 2008). Characteristics associated with effective programs include (1) targeted populations, (2) intensive services, (3) a focus on behavior, (4) inclusion of both parents and children, and (5) program fidelity. Although the gulf between EBPs and everyday child-welfare practice is large at present, policymakers have been recommending EBPs as both clinically and economically wise investments (APA, 2009; Cohen et al., 2006; Kauffman Best Practices Project, 2004; Lee et al., 2008). Forensic evaluators need to be aware of the potential for effective interventions so they can recommend service components likely to meet families' needs. However, they also should be mindful that access to high-quality services is scarce.

Conceptual Frameworks of Parenting and Child Maltreatment

Parenting is essential to human life, yet so basic that it defies easy description. Parenting involves being the primary provider of a child's physical care, nurturance, development, learning, and emotional well-being, with its attendant rewards and despite whatever difficulties and personal sacrifices that commitment may entail. Scholars (cf. Bornstein, 2002; National Research Council and Institute of Medicine, 2000) have developed numerous frameworks to conceptualize parenting and parent–child relationships, and several of these models have been applied to child maltreatment (e.g., Rogosch et al., 2002; Wolfe, 1999). The theoretical roots of various frameworks reflect psychodynamic, behavioral, cognitive, sociological, ethological, and ecological systems perspectives. Contemporary research suggests that no one theory holds preeminence in under-

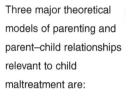

INFO

Three major theoretical models of parenting and parent–child relationships relevant to child maltreatment are:

- Attachment theory
- Dimensions of parenting style theory
- Ecological systems theory

standing parenting and child maltreatment, but rather that multiple explanations are open to study and potential integration. Three theoretical models of parenting and parent–child relationships (attachment theory, a dimensional theory of parenting style, and ecological systems theory) that have figured prominently in research are described briefly in the sections that follow. Although some models initially targeted the mother as the primary parent, they have been expanded to include the father or other major caregivers. Following a description of the three models, the influence of culture on parenting is discussed.

Attachment Theory

Bowlby (1969/1982) proposed that infants are predisposed to a set of built-in behaviors that keep the caregiver nearby to protect the child and promote survival. "Attachment behavior" (crying, seeking proximity with a caregiver) in response to fearful stimuli is seen as a biologically adaptive response. Bowlby theorized that attachment develops during the first year of life when the parent provides an infant with predictable, sensitive responses to the child's cues and needs. This "secure base" provides reassurance and allows the child to confidently explore the environment. As children develop, attachment promotes the development of strong affectionate ties for specific people who have responded to one's needs and with whom one experiences pleasure and comfort (Berk, 2008).

Ainsworth and colleagues (Ainsworth et al., 1978) developed a method of assessing infants' responses to brief maternal separation in a laboratory setting in order to classify the quality of attachment as "secure" or "insecure." A child who, at reunion with the mother, goes to her, greets her positively, and then settles down and resumes play is classified as secure. A child who remains detached or is angry and yet clingy at reunion is classified as insecure. Research on middle-class American families has indicated that about 60% of infants show secure attachment, while others show various forms of insecurity. Numerous factors, such as the quality of caregiving, infant characteristics, family stressors, and the parent's own history of attachment experiences, influence parent–child attachment relationships. Children with insecure attachments have been shown to have less positive adjustment than those with secure attachment, and insecure attachment is considered a risk factor for later psychological problems (Berk, 2008; National Research Council and Institute of Medicine, 2000).

Attachment theory posits that physically abusive and neglectful parents would display less positive and responsive behavior toward their children compared to non-maltreating parents, and research supports this presumption (Cassidy & Mohr, 2001). Some physically abused children do not fit typical organized patterns of insecurity but rather display chaotic, disorganized responses (e.g., freezing, disorientation) to their caregivers (Crittenden & Ainsworth, 1989). This disorganized pattern is considered of major concern for treatment due to emerging evidence of a strong link between disorganized attachment and risk for psychopathology (Cassidy & Mohr, 2001; Cicchetti, Rogosch, & Toth, 2006). Recent EBPs with children and parents or foster parents have shown positive changes in attachment following intervention, suggesting that the negative effects of maladaptive early parenting experiences are open to change (Cicchetti et al., 2006; Dozier et al., 2006).

Dimensions of Parenting Style

Baumrind (1971) and other developmental researchers (e.g., Maccoby & Martin, 1983) studied the concept of parenting style by measuring two central traits of parenting: demandingness (control, strictness, and supervision) and responsiveness (warmth, sensitivity, autonomy-granting). According to this conceptualization, parents are classified into one of four quadrants: *authoritative* (high in both demandingness and responsiveness), *authoritarian* (high in demandingness and low in responsiveness), *indulgent* (low in demandingness but responsive), or *uninvolved* (low in both demandingness and responsiveness). In longitudinal research, an authoritative parent style (a balance of emotional affection and adaptive firmness) has been associated with more competent, academically successful, and problem-free children than the other groups (Baumrind, 1991). Research suggests that these results are most characteristic of European American samples, and that authoritativeness has been less predictive of outcomes for ethnic minority youth (Chao, 1994; Darling & Steinberg, 1993).

Much of the research on parenting styles has been conducted with normative, middle-class families. Nevertheless, Baumrind's conceptualization of parenting style is relevant in considering the interactions implicated in child maltreatment. Physical child abuse is thought to arise out of interactions in which parents respond to perceived child misbehavior with inconsistent, ineffective, and coercive behavior, which escalates into abuse. Neglect is presumed to relate to chronically detached, uninterested, and inconsistent parenting. Theoretically, parent–child interactions involving physically abusive or neglectful parenting fit within the extremes of Baumrind's authoritarian and uninvolved styles, respectively. The static dimensions of parenting style are influenced dynamically by contributions from the child and the environment, and thus parenting style is most useful as a framework for characterizing general

3 chapter

INFO

The four classifications of parenting style are:

- Authoritative
- Authoritarian
- Indulgent
- Uninvolved

parent–child relationships. Research from observational studies of maltreating and non-maltreating parents (described later in this chapter) demonstrate differences in observed levels of parent–child interactions consistent with expectations from a parenting style conceptualization (Wilson Rack, Shi, & Norris, 2008).

One widely debated research topic pertinent to authoritarian parenting concerns the impact of corporal punishment, the most identifiable form of parental control, on children (Aucion, Frick, & Bodin, 2006; Gershoff, 2002; Larzelere, 2000). The adverse effects of severe corporal punishment have been well documented; however, debate continues on the threshold of punishment that results in lasting emotional harm, and on whether the negative effects of moderate corporal punishment are minimized in the context of positive parenting practices. A related area of study is psychological control, which has been distinguished from behavioral control. Whereas *behavioral control* refers to attempts (such as spanking or firm commands) to manage the child's behavior, *psychological control* refers to behaviors that potentially intrude on the child's psychological or emotional development through shaming, withdrawal of love, guilt induction, or other manipulative strategies (Barber, 1996). Severe forms of psychological control fit with the definition of psychological or emotional maltreatment. Research has indicated that psychological control has detrimental effects on children, more so than strict behavioral discipline (Barber, 2002).

EBPs designed to strengthen behaviors consistent with authoritative parenting have been shown to be effective with maltreated children. These programs are directed at training parents in positive interactions and consistent, nonviolent discipline techniques. For example, evidence-based parent-training programs have demonstrated success at preventing child maltreatment (Prinz et al., 2009) and at reducing recurrences of maltreatment for physically abusive parents (Chaffin et al., 2004).

Ecological Systems Theory

In Bronfenbrenner's (1979) ecological systems theory, the child is viewed as developing within a multilevel system of relationships, behavior settings, and community contexts. This integrative model conceptualizes human development as a product of interactions among the individual, the environment, and the linkages occurring at different levels. Belsky (1993), among others, has applied Bronfenbrenner's ecological model to an analysis of the etiology of child maltreatment, emphasizing the contribution of several independent factors. One set is individual factors such as characteristics of the child (e.g., young age, developmental delays, or behavior problems) or the parent (e.g., depression, unrealistic expectations of the child, or a history of having been abused as a child). A second set of factors is associated with the interaction between the parent and child in the immediate context of caregiving, such as the parent's responsiveness to the child's prosocial behavior, reliance on punitive control strategies, or emotional arousal in the context of child misbehavior. (The interactive set of factors is the primary focus of the attachment and parenting style models described above.) A third set of factors relates to the broader context in which parenting and child development are embedded, including community (e.g., social support), cultural (e.g., prevailing attitudes about corporal punishment and violence), and historical, evolutionary factors (e.g., biologically driven conflicts between parent and child under conditions of scarce resources). Of these factors, the evolutionary context is the most controversial one (Baumrind, 1995) and the one least open to empirical study.

Belsky's model posits that child maltreatment is determined by the balance of stressors and supports, or risks and protective factors, at any point in time. Although research supports numerous parent, child, and environmental factors as potential etiological variables, most of the research compares groups of parents on only one variable or factor at a time. For example, parents with major mental illness are likely to encounter challenges that could preclude adequate caregiving (Nicholson, Sweeney, & Geller, 1998a and 1998b), yet many parents with mental illness are able to care for their children on their own or with support (Ostler, 2008). To understand how and when mental illness compromises parenting requires an assessment of the interaction of this factor with others in increasing the likelihood of maltreatment. An ecological model suggests that there are many pathways to child abuse and neglect, but also that there are many potential approaches to intervention. Further, because of the multi-determined nature of child maltreatment, an ecological model presumes that treatments directed at any single factor are likely to be insufficient (Belsky, 1993). Some EBPs target multiple risk factors. For example, treatment for children exposed to trauma may include interventions directed at the children and their parents, and actions to enhance the safety of the family environment (Cohen et al., 2006).

Cultural Factors Affecting Parenting

All cultures have rules concerning appropriate and inappropriate conduct with children, but beliefs may vary widely regarding what is condoned (Korbin, 1981; 1997). Some behaviors (such as beating children or threatening to abandon them) that are viewed as excessively harsh in most Western cultures are accepted as normative in others (Collier et al., 1999; Hong & Hong, 1991). Contextual factors such as racial or ethnic background, region of the country, religiosity, socio-economic status, and a parent's own experiences of childrearing influence parenting beliefs and practices (Darling & Steinberg, 1993; Harkness & Super, 1996; Kotchick & Forehand, 2002). Further, the impact of parenting behaviors on children's adjustment has been found to differ depending on the contexts in which these behaviors are situated. To the extent that parents' punitive discipline practices are culturally normative, they may be seen by children as less rejecting and have a less negative impact on children (Lansford et al., 2005).

Cultural differences in parenting practices are important in forensic mental health assessment. Much of the research on parenting and child development has been conducted in the United States and has involved largely middle-class, European American families. Therefore, a basic question arises as to whether the principles and findings drawn from this research hold true across cultures, and, particularly for the current discussion, whether they apply to families involved in the child maltreatment system, who often are poor or ethnic minorities. Behavioral research provides a

conceptual base for viewing
parent–child relationships and
potential risk and protective factors; nevertheless, it is crucial
that professionals conducting
FMHAs take into account the
cultural background and context of the individual family in a

BEST PRACTICE

It is crucial to take into account a
family's cultural background when
conducting a parenting capacity
evaluation. Practices that may be
frowned upon in the United States may
be accepted as normal in other cultures.

parenting capacity evaluation. It is also important for evaluators to
gain competence about culturally diverse parenting practices and
to seek consultation when evaluating families from cultures outside
their own experience.

It is easy to see how evaluators could interpret some parenting
as less desirable mainly on the grounds that it differs from their
own experience and appears detrimental from their perspective.
Consider, for example, parents who choose to discriminate openly
between their children according to gender, or who teach their
children racist views. As Levesque (2000) noted, these practices
may be unpopular or morally repugnant to some, but they are
permissible within the wide latitude given parents under the
Constitution. Similarly, Azar and Goff (2007) cautioned about the
potential for misinterpretation when observing parents from a
group different than one's own. The observer "might perceive
'harsh' words about a child as a 'lack of bonding' or an example of
'rejecting the child,' when in reality such 'harshness' does not
evoke the same feelings in the parent's cultural group, and more
importantly, is not seen negatively by the child from that cultural
group" (Azar & Goff, 2007, p. 551).

Another reason cultural differences in parenting are important
in conducting FMHAs relates to the interpretation of what constitutes maltreatment. Researchers, lawyers, and child welfare professionals have struggled with where to draw the line between
physical discipline and physical abuse, particularly when it is seen
in a cultural context (Lansford et al., 2005; Whipple & Richey,
1997). Some behaviors, such as burn marks intended as folk rituals
for medical symptoms, may be viewed as culturally accepted in one
context but become problematic when parents engage in them

BEST PRACTICE
You can help the court by providing possible explanations for culturally controversial practices based on research, cultural expertise, or parenting assessment.

outside of their normative context (Hansen, 1997). When families immigrate to the United States, they may engage in practices that were culturally accepted in the family's homeland but that meet American definitions of child abuse or neglect (Gray & Cosgrove, 1985; Levesque, 2000). In some cases these practices are motivated by a desire to socialize the child into the family's culture and result in no long-term harm. On the other hand, behaviors that involve severe punishment, public degradation of the child, or other questionable practices may be viewed as abusive even if they are normative in the family's culture.

Evaluators in parenting capacity evaluations are in a position to shed light on the nature of and possible explanations for culturally controversial practices, regardless of whether the actions have been determined by the court to be abusive. They can do this by seeking information regarding (1) the intensity, severity, and context of the parent's behavior; (2) the child's perceptions of his or her treatment and evidence of emotional harm; and (3) the parent's intentions and beliefs about the actions in relation to socialization goals of the family's culture (Korbin, 1981, 1997; Whipple & Richey, 1997).

Research on Assessment Measures Used in Forensic Practice

In comparison to the voluminous research on parenting, child development, and child maltreatment, the research base in forensic assessment is relatively recent and decidedly smaller. Heilbrun, Rogers, and Otto (2002) defined three categories of structured assessment tools and procedures used in forensic assessment. They consist of *clinical* measures (methods initially developed for assessment, diagnosis, and treatment-planning in a therapeutic context); *forensically relevant* measures (methods to assess clinical constructs most relevant to persons involved in the legal system, such as risk of violence or response style); and *forensic assessment* measures (methods specifically designed to assess psycholegal capacities). Melton and colleagues (2007, p. 48) concluded that, across all areas of forensic assessment, clinical assessment measures are the least likely of these three categories to be helpful in the forensic context because they assess general psychological constructs (e.g., intelligence, personality, mood, or academic achievement) that are only loosely related to the psycholegal issues of interest. By contrast, forensically relevant instruments and forensic assessment instruments are,

> **INFO**
>
> There are three categories of structured assessment tools and procedures used in forensic assessment:
>
> 1. Clinical measures
> 2. Forensically relevant measures
> 3. Forensic assessment measures

by their nature, more directly related to the issues of individuals involved in the legal system and thus may be beneficial, providing they are well validated.

The following sections summarize research on assessment approaches relevant to parenting capacity evaluations. To complement the small research base, reviews of measures in other forensic areas are included to reflect current recommendations and issues to consider in selecting assessment approaches. Topics covered are (1) general psychological measures; (2) parenting-specific measures; and (3) methods of observing parent–child interactions. (This section focuses on forensic research and reviews of tests; reference citations to test manuals are provided in Chapter 5.)

Research on General Psychological Measures with Parents

The forensic literature reflects varying opinions on the utility of general psychological measures in forensic practice; however, for the most part, the literature has not focused on parents undergoing evaluation in child protection cases. Some writers (e.g., Grisso, 1986, 2003; Heilbrun, Grisso, & Goldstein, 2009) have agreed with Melton et al. (2007) that clinical measures of psychopathology, intelligence, or personality are too general to address psycholegal questions regarding functional capabilities and deficits. Nevertheless, these authorities noted that traditional measures can be helpful in explaining why an individual is or is not competent. As discussed in Chapter 2, mental illness and mental impairment may undergird two of the statutory grounds for termination of parental rights, when these conditions are shown to interfere with minimally adequate parenting. Furthermore, traditional measures may reveal response styles useful in assessing the validity of test data. Evolving evidentiary standards increasingly have emphasized the importance of scientific reliability and legal relevance of the testing used in forensic assessment (Heilbrun et al., 2009). One index of a test's acceptability in court is the profession's view of the instrument.

Standardized intellectual and achievement tests are commonly used when questions arise as to an individual's general cognitive functioning. In surveys of forensic evaluators, the Wechsler Intelligence Scales have been viewed as popular and endorsed across a wide range of forensic areas (Archer et al., 2006; Lally, 2003). Less frequently used but generally accepted were the Stanford-Binet–Revised (Lally, 2003) and the Wide Range Achievement Test–3 (Archer et al., 2006). The performance-based nature of cognitive tests and their objective scoring criteria have been cited as positive features in forensic assessment reviews (e.g., Medoff, 2003).

In contrast to the general acceptance of standardized cognitive tests in forensic assessment, critiques of personality measures have varied in their conclusions. In one survey of forensic psychologists, the Minnesota Multiphasic Personality Inventory 2 (MMPI-2), the Personality Assessment Inventory (PAI), and the Millon Clinical Multiaxial Inventory III (MCMI-III) were cited as the most frequently used and generally acceptable personality tests (Archer et al., 2006). However, in another survey, the MMPI-2 and PAI were rated "acceptable," whereas the MCMI-III was rated "equivocal" (Lally, 2003). Criticism of the MCMI-III has been

INFO

Although commonly viewed as too general for use in forensic assessment, some clinical measures, such as the Wechsler Intelligence Scales, may be useful for addressing competence.

that the test is deficient with respect to criterion-related and construct validity for Axis II disorders (Rogers, Salekin, & Sewell, 1999), there is a lack of clear evidence that the test meets scientific and evidentiary standards (Erickson, Lilienfeld, & Vitacco, 2007), the test was not normed on a population that included normal adults and hence does not allow for comparisons between subjects that are patients and the normal population, and the test may over-pathologize subjects (Craig, 2006). With respect to a child protection setting, Dyer (1999, p. 99) recommended both the MCMI-II and MCMI-III as useful in termination-of-rights cases in order to assess "core personality dysfunctions" related to the "parents' chronic failings." However, no research has examined the relationship between MCMI profiles and parenting functioning. Data supporting such a relationship would provide an empirical basis for such a recommendation.

A frequent concern in using psychological measures with court-involved individuals is that the tests' accuracy may be reduced by response distortions. Of relevance in parenting capacity evaluations is the likelihood that parents will under-report symptoms or over-report positive qualities in order to appear well adjusted. In one of few studies conducted on parents undergoing forensic evaluation in the child protection system, Carr, Moretti, and Cue (2005) examined the validity of MMPI-2 and PAI profiles in evaluations regarding termination of parental rights. Participants were 91 mothers and 73 fathers in court-ordered evaluations. Their findings indicated that 41% of parents had t scores ≥ 65 on the L scale and 20% had t scores ≥ 65 on the K scale. Using a t score cutoff of 70, 27% of the profiles were elevated on the L scale and 6% on the K scale. Furthermore, Carr et al. (2005) reported that elevated L and/or K scale scores were associated with lower scores on some of the MMPI-2 clinical scales, suggesting a suppressive effect. They noted that the suppressive effect on clinical scale scores with the current sample was more exaggerated than in research with custody litigants. Elevations on the PAI validity scales in Carr et al.'s sample were considerably less frequent; however, validity scale elevations on the MMPI-2 were correlated significantly with validity scale scores on the PAI and the Child Abuse

Potential Inventory, a measure of attitudes about childrearing (the CAPI is discussed further in the next section). Carr and colleagues concluded that their data demonstrated "a pervasive problem of positive self-presentation bias in compromising the validity of test results in this population" (p. 188).

In a further investigation of validity issues, Stredny, Archer, and Mason (2006) examined the MMPI-2 and MCMI-III scores of 127 parents undergoing parental competency evaluations. Similarly to Carr et al. (2005), the Stredny et al. sample produced mean MMPI-2 elevations on the L scale that were substantially higher than on the K scale. They also produced an elevated mean value on the MCMI-III Desirability (Y) scale, generally consistent with the defensiveness seen on the MMPI-2 L scale. Unlike Carr et al. (2005), Stredny et al. (2006) found that the standard scale findings of their sample on both the MMPI-2 and MCMI-III were consistent with previous research on child custody litigants.

These two studies are in keeping with evidence from other research that the demands of court-ordered testing situations are likely to contribute to parents' motivation to present themselves positively. However, rather than viewing positive presentation bias as a basis for invalidating test results (cf. Carr et al., 2005), Ben-Porath (2009) proposed that evaluators consider the pattern as typical under the circumstances. Ben-Porath noted that L-scale elevations on the MMPI-2 are more common with low socioeconomic samples and those from highly religious or traditional homes. For these reasons, he recommended that MMPI-2 clinical scale scores can still be interpreted when L-scale t score elevations are in the range of 65–79, keeping in mind the possible effects on clinical scale scores. Issues regarding the validity of tests are discussed further in Chapters 5 and 6.

BEWARE
Parents undergoing compulsory evaluations are likely to over-report positive qualities and under-report negative ones, which can lead to invalid test results.

In addition to objective scales of personality, projective scales of personality such as the Rorschach Inkblot Method, the Thematic Apperception Test, sentence-completion forms, and projective drawings have a long history of use in the field of psychology. Projective tests were reviewed as lacking reliability and validity and therefore as inappropriate for use in child custody evaluations (Erickson et al., 2007). Lally (2003) found that, in a survey of forensic evaluators, tests of this design generally were rated as "unacceptable." Although the Rorschach was not rated as negatively as other projective measures, it was still rated "unacceptable" by the majority of the evaluators surveyed. Other reviewers (Erard, 2007; Medoff, 2003), however, endorsed the Rorschach as a scientifically based assessment technique when scored with Exner's Comprehensive System. There is considerable and heated debate in the literature about the validity of the Rorschach scoring system and the normative sample it is based on (Garb et al., 2005), leading to controversy about the appropriateness of using the Rorschach Inkblot Method in forensic settings.

In summary, general psychological measures have been viewed as having varying levels of applicability to forensic assessment. Although some writers have claimed that psychological tests can address areas of functioning specific to parental capabilities (Medoff, 2003), evidence is lacking to interpret performance on general psychological measures as directly indicative of parenting abilities or deficits. No studies yet have examined the relationship of general psychological measures to parenting functioning of individuals undergoing FMHA in a child protection setting.

Research on Parenting-Specific Measures

Tests of parenting-related constructs are designed to tap functional characteristics; i.e., knowledge, attitudes, beliefs, and behaviors related to childrearing. Literally hundreds of parenting-specific measures have been developed for research or clinical purposes, yet few were designed to examine the lower end of parenting capabilities. Otto and Edens (2003) identified 34 instruments related to parenting, a few of which were developed for use in forensic assessments and others of which are primarily research scales. Their list includes evaluator ratings of parents' competence in various areas, parental self-report questionnaires, observational measures of parent–child interactions, parent measures of stress in raising children, and risk assessments. Of these, Otto and Edens selected

INFO

The following parent-specific measures are used frequently in child protection evaluations:

● The Parent Awareness Skills Survey (PASS)

● The Parent Perception of Child Profile (PPCP)

● The Parent–Child Relationship Inventory (PCRI)

● The Parenting Stress Index (PSI)

● The Child Abuse Potential Inventory (CAPI)

five measures used frequently by forensic practitioners in child protection evaluations for more detailed review. These five measures are examined briefly in the sections that follow.

Two measures, the Parent Awareness Skills Survey (PASS) (Bricklin, 1990) and the Parent Perception of Child Profile (PPCP) (Bricklin & Elliott, 1991), were developed as clinical tools for use in child custody and child protection evaluations. The PASS is a series of childcare scenarios presented and discussed with parents to assess their understanding of how to handle typical responsibilities. The PPCP assesses parents' awareness and understanding of child development across various stages. Both measures include face-valid samples of functional parenting abilities that potentially provide useful information germane to parenting capacity evaluations (Otto & Edens, 2003). However, there is no evidence of an empirical basis for the development or scoring methods used, no norms, and no research on the reliability or validity of the measures. Thus, although they appear to have potential relevance to parenting capacity evaluations, reviewers have found that these measures (as well as other measures developed by Bricklin) do not meet scientific and evidentiary standards for family court evaluations (Erickson et al., 2007; Melton et al., 2007; Otto & Edens, 2003).

The Parent–Child Relationship Inventory (PCRI) (Gerard, 1994) is a self-report questionnaire of parents' attitudes toward parenting and their children. The PCRI contains seven content scales (such as parental support, satisfaction with parenting, and involvement) and two validity indicators (social desirability and inconsistency). Reviews of the PCRI (Boothroyd, 2004; Marchant & Paulson, 2004) described systematic and comprehensive psychometric development as well as standardized scores based on a normative sample of parents identified through schools and daycares; however, these reviewers found limited research on the PCRI with at-risk parents. Otto and Edens (2003) concluded that use of the PCRI in forensic evaluations of parents was speculative, due to the absence of data on its usefulness in classifying parents with better or worse parenting abilities or in predicting child outcomes.

The Parenting Stress Index (PSI) (Abidin, 1995) is a self-report questionnaire of a parent's experience of stress in the context of the parent–child relationship. Both the PSI and a newer short form (PSI-SF) contain subscales assessing parental distress, aspects of the parent–child relationship, and the parent's view of the child. Both versions also have a defensiveness scale. As Otto and Edens (2003) summarized, the PSI is reasonably sound psychometrically and has been subjected to extensive research with at-risk populations. PSI scores have been shown to correlate with outcomes of interest to forensic evaluators, including sensitivity to intervention and ability to differentiate between maltreating and non-maltreating parents. Limitations of the PSI relate to concerns with its factor structure and the composition of the normative sample. Based on its overall strengths, Otto and Edens recommended the PSI as a useful measure in parenting capacity evaluations.

The Child Abuse Potential Inventory (CAPI) (Milner, 1986) is a forced-choice, agree-disagree questionnaire to screen characteristics and attitudes associated with physical child abuse. The measure yields an overall abuse scale with an established cutoff to indicate that the respondent has characteristics similar to those of known physical child abusers. Validity scales are used to produce three response-distortion indexes (faking good, faking bad, and random response). Considerable psychometric research supports the measure's reliability as well as its concurrent and criterion validity (Milner, 1986, 1990, 1994). The CAPI's predictive validity (Milner et al., 1984) was investigated with 200 participants enrolled in a treatment program for parents at risk for physical abuse.

3
chapter

CAPI scores at pretreatment accurately predicted all parents who abused their child within the subsequent six months; however, only 11% of parents with pretreatment scores above the cutoff engaged in abuse. The large (89%) false positive rate indicates that caution is needed in interpreting CAPI scores. Although the CAPI was not designed to measure parenting abilities, its extensive research with at-risk populations and ability to detect parents who are at higher risk to abuse their children are unique strengths. Otto and Edens (2003) recommended use of the CAPI as one means of identifying parents at risk of repeated abuse in forensic assessments. One caveat in use of the CAPI is that it is not an appropriate measure of sexual-abuse risk, as it was designed to assess physical-abuse risk.

A survey of forensic psychologists' test usage (Archer et al., 2006) included four parenting-specific measures for child-related forensic issues (non-custody specific measures). The most frequently used test was the PSI, followed by the CAPI, the PCRI, and the Stress Index for Parents of Adolescentst (SIPA), respectively. Yanez and Fremouw (2004), using the *Daubert* guidelines, specifically assessed the PSI, CAPI, and PCRI with regard to their usefulness in assessing parents in adoption, child custody, and parental fitness cases. Yanez and Fremouw (2004) concluded that the CAPI met all four *Daubert* criteria, and that the PSI met or marginally met the criteria. They determined that the PCRI was below acceptable levels on all criteria.

In summary, despite the plethora of clinical and research measures assessing parenting attitudes and behaviors, only two, the PSI and the CAPI, have been recommended in forensic reviews as appropriate for FMHAs in child protection cases. A few other instruments have been subjected to empirical evaluation, and the evidence at present is not sufficient to recommend their widespread use in FMHA. For example, the Adult-Adolescent Parenting Inventory (AAPI, Bavolek, 1984), the more recent AAPI 2 (Bavolek & Keene, 1999), and the Parent Opinion Questionnaire (POQ, Azar et al., 1984) could potentially provide useful clinical information as part of a multi-method assessment process. However, given psychometric and validity concerns regarding the

AAPI (Lutenbacher, 2001), AAPI 2 (Conners et al., 2006), and POQ (Haskett et al., 2006), forensic evaluators should use extreme caution in interpreting parents' scores on these instruments in parenting capacity evaluations. Of particular concern are parent-related measures without strong validity scales, since any forensic examinee is potentially defensive in responding, given the high stakes involved. Research (Milner & Crouch, 1997; Moretti, Carr, & Schoular, 1999, cited in Carr et al., 2005) has found that at-risk parents were capable of "faking good" on the AAPI, which would obviate its usefulness in identifying parents at risk. Similarly, no differences were found between maltreating and non-maltreating parents in an independent investigation of the POQ (Haskett et al., 2006). Thus, these measures may be useful mainly in identifying parents with extreme scores or in identifying items for further discussion with parents.

INFO

Only the PSI and the CAPI have been recommended in forensic reviews as appropriate parenting-specific measures for assessments in child protection cases.

3
chapter

Methods of Observing Parent–Child Interactions

The most direct source of information about parenting behavior comes from observation of parent–child interactions. Given that parent self-reports can be influenced by social desirability bias, observational methods provide an independent source of data about parenting in samples undergoing court evaluation. Direct observation offers a sample of functional parenting skills and deficits under conditions when parents presumably are attempting to demonstrate their best caregiving skills (Budd, 2001). Observations also provide information on the child's functioning, strengths, needs, and responsiveness in the parent's presence. Data on both functional parenting abilities and child needs are essential to assessing the nexus between parenting capabilities and childrearing demands.

BEST PRACTICE
Parent self-reports should be augmented with parent–child behavioral observations in order to get a clearer picture of the individual's parenting abilities.

Numerous methods for assessing parenting-related constructs exist; however, no current observational measures fulfill all the criteria to qualify as formal forensic measures (Otto & Edens, 2003). To do so would require that the measures be designed or adapted for forensic purposes, that standardized administration and scoring procedures exist, and that their reliability and validity have been established with parents in a child protection context. The diversity of settings; numbers, ages, and characteristics of children; and conditions under which parent–child observation occurs in FMHAs makes standardization of observational procedures particularly challenging. Instead, some (e.g., Budd, 2001; Pezzot-Pearce & Pearce, 2004; Schmidt et al., 2007) have provided guidelines for informal observation of parent–child interactions during parenting capacity evaluations.

A recent meta-analysis examined the nature and extent of differences in parent communication styles during parent–child observation with maltreatment samples. Wilson et al. (2008) analyzed 33 observational studies comparing physically abusive, neglectful, and non-maltreating parents during interactions with their children. To be eligible for inclusion, studies needed to include a sample of parents with a documented history of child maltreatment and a demographically matched comparison sample of non-maltreating parents. Three clusters of parent behavior were analyzed: aversiveness (e.g., anger, disapproval); involvement (e.g., questions, responsiveness); and positivity (e.g., laughter, praise). Across studies, differences between maltreating and non-maltreating parents were medium in effect size ($d = .46$ to $.52$). Physically abusive parents were distinguished from non-maltreating parents in terms of higher rates of aversive behavior, whereas neglectful parents were distinguished from non-maltreating parents in terms of lower rates of involvement. Both abusive and neglectful samples displayed significantly lower rates of positivity compared non-maltreating samples.

Wilson and colleagues (2008) found that several variables moderated the magnitude, though not the direction, of observed differences. Specifically, studies obtained larger effects when families were observed for longer periods of time (e.g., over an hour), with younger children (under five years), and in the home rather than in a laboratory setting. The authors classified the task structure of interactions into four categories, from highly structured (e.g., researcher tells the parents what tasks to do, what objects to use, and how to use these objects) to unstructured (e.g., no rules, such as free play). Task structure was a moderator for parent involvement, such that studies using unstructured tasks found larger differences between maltreating and non-maltreating parents than did those using only highly structured tasks.

Wilson and colleagues' (2008) meta-analysis has several practical implications for use of parent–child observation in parenting capacity evaluations. First, the findings provide support for observing behavioral instances of the categories of aversiveness, involvement, and positivity. Second, they imply the value of observing for longer periods of time (i.e., an hour or more) and in naturalistic settings when possible. Third, they suggest that parent–child observation may be a more useful method for assessing parenting behaviors with younger children than older children. Finally, the findings regarding task structure indicate that it is advisable to have parents and children complete both unstructured and structured, as opposed to only structured tasks, in order to allow for a greater observable range of parental involvement.

Research on Forensic Assessment Practice

Little systematic information exists on typical forensic evaluation practice or on how judges and child protection agencies use the resultant reports. One exception is a series of studies carried out in the child protection division of a large, urban juvenile court system serving metropolitan Chicago. After a comprehensive investigation confirmed extensive problems in the content and quality of forensic practice (Budd et al., 2002; Budd et al., 2001), researchers collaborated with court professionals to design and implement a multidisciplinary reform. The reform model was developed for use in both child protection and juvenile justice divisions (Kavanaugh et al., 2006; Scally et al., 2001–2002), although only the child protection side is relevant here. This research focused on a single county's system (Cook County), so its results may not be representative of other jurisdictions. Still, it provides an example of both the problems and the prospects of forensic assessment in child protection proceedings. The next few paragraphs describe highlights of the Cook County research on parenting capacity evaluations and two independent studies. One additional study (Budd & Springman, in press) examined the types of referral issues precipitating requests for evaluations of parents and the extent to which evaluators provided recommendations regarding ultimate issues in evaluations of parents; relevant findings are described in later chapters in this volume.

Budd and colleagues (2001) examined 190 randomly selected evaluations completed on parents and coded the reports on criteria recommended in the forensic literature. They documented numerous substantive shortcomings in relation to recommended practice. For example, evaluations of parents typically were completed in a single session in an office or clinic, used few if any sources of information other than the parent, often cited no previous records, rarely used behavioral methods, stated purposes in general rather than specific terms, emphasized weaknesses over strengths in reporting results, and often neglected to describe the parent's caregiving qualities or the child's relationship with the parent. Further, Budd et al. (2001) found that evaluations relied heavily on traditional psychological instruments not directly related to parenting (e.g., cognitive tests, objective and projective personality measures), and most failed to state whether parents were warned of the evaluation's purpose and limits of confidentiality. Moretti and colleagues (2003) reported some of these same shortcomings in their unpublished study of parenting capacity evaluations in Canada.

Another study (Conley, 2003–2004) of parenting capacity evaluations examined 24 randomly selected

INFO

A series of studies of forensic reports produced by evaluators working in a child protection system in Chicago found numerous shortcomings. Reports showed that many evaluators did not follow recommended practices, supporting the need for more training.

assessments completed in Australia to assist the court and parties in child welfare case planning. Conley noted three areas of concern. First, a substantial emphasis was placed on traditional psychological measures (intelligence and objective personality tests) to determine the presence or absence of mental health problems in parents. Second, most assessors appeared to lack knowledge about parent–child attachment relationships and used insufficient methods to gather data about attachment. Finally, Conley reported that assessors lacked a framework in which to analyze their findings and data. These qualitative findings, although different in some details than Budd et al. (2001), suggest the need for further research and training to improve the quality of evaluations in child protection.

Another study by Budd and colleagues (Budd et al., 2004) investigated the link between evaluations and legal decisions. They reviewed court records associated with 171 randomly selected mental health evaluations completed on parents (by either a court-based clinic or community evaluators) and 44 evaluations completed on children. Reviewers examined court orders (e.g., no-contact orders, visitation orders, or permanency determinations) for evidence that the decision was based on the evaluation (e.g., a permanency order that referred to the evaluation as the reason for the change in goal from "return home" to "adoption," or a motion that requested unsupervised visits and quoted the evaluation as evidence of the mother's progress, followed a few months later by an order granting unsupervised visits). They found that evaluations were cited as a basis for 36% of court-based parent evaluations, 21% of non–court-based parent evaluations, and 2% of child evaluations. Budd et al. (2004, p. 638) concluded that their study suggested a modest impact of parent evaluations on legal decisions and notably less impact for child evaluations. They noted that child evaluations may be conducted mainly for use in service planning and thus have less bearing on court decisions.

A multi-disciplinary team of researchers and professionals in Cook County designed a comprehensive model for reform based on the problems identified with the evaluation process (Scally et al., 2001-2002). They then conducted a three-year pilot study of the model prior to its full-scale implementation (Budd et al., 2006).

The reform model addressed three key areas for change: (a) problems in the process of acquiring clinical information (e.g., vague referral questions, repeated and unnecessary evaluations, lack of timeliness); (b) poor content and quality of the clinical information obtained; and (c) system-wide constraints (e.g., varying practices among courtrooms, general lack of knowledge among attorneys of what constitutes a competent evaluation, poor communication). Core features of the model included establishing liaisons between the court and clinical providers; creating a structured system for focusing, screening, and responding to requests for evaluations; training for clinicians in "best practice" methods of forensic assessment; and educating court personnel about the population and what to expect in forensic assessments (Scally et al., 2001–2002).

Budd and colleagues (2006) studied the effectiveness of the model by comparing parent evaluations completed by the pilot court clinic with those of three other provider sources in terms of criteria recommended in the forensic literature. Overall, evaluations conducted by the pilot clinic demonstrated a high proportion of recommended features, including multiple sessions, settings, and sources; parent–child observation; articulation of specific referral issues; warning on limits of confidentiality; reference to reliability and validity; and description of findings regarding parenting strengths, weaknesses, and relationship to the child. Furthermore, the pilot clinic completed evaluations promptly and consistently in relation to other groups. In short, the findings suggested greater use of recommended practices and more timely, consistent reports by the pilot clinic. Given the quasi-experimental nature of the study (i.e., the lack of randomized assignment of cases to provider groups), the research could not ascertain whether the pilot clinic's superior performance was due to the reform model, but several of its features were aimed at the observed changes. At the completion of the study, Cook County adopted the pilot model court-wide through the creation of the Cook County Juvenile Court Clinic (Kavanaugh et al., 2006).

The small research literature on forensic practice in child protection cases sheds light on the shortcomings characterizing parenting capacity evaluations in at least some settings. Although limited in its generalizability, the findings underscore the need to educate MHPs and courts about what to expect in forensic assessments. The promising results of Cook County's reform model suggest that concerted change efforts can bring about meaningful improvements in the quality of FMHAs.

Summary

The research reviewed in this chapter confirms that child abuse and neglect are persistent in our society. Numerous parent, child, family, and environmental factors can impact the parent–child relationship and negatively affect a parent's caregiving capacity, thereby placing a child at risk of harm. Services designed to assist victims of child maltreatment and rehabilitate families are inadequate and often ineffective. Despite extensive challenges, there are signs of increased attention to and support for evidence-based interventions that can improve child welfare practice.

> **3**
> chapter

Conceptual models such as attachment theory, dimensions of parenting style, and ecological systems theory provide useful frameworks for considering how parenting can go awry in case of child maltreatment. Cultural factors influence parenting beliefs and practices, and evaluators need to be sensitive to the subtle impact of their own cultural lens in conducting FMHAs. General psychological assessment measures, parenting-specific measures, and observational methods have, for the most part, not been designed for or tested with families in the child protection system. As a result, little is known about the validity of methods for parenting capacity evaluations. It often is difficult to unravel the effects of poor parenting from the iatrogenic effects of the family's involvement in the child protection system, poverty, or other life stressors on parents and parent–child relationships. Although few studies have examined forensic measures or forensic assessment practice in a child protection context, a small literature is now available to provide direction in planning and conducting evaluations.

APPLICATION

Preparation for the Evaluation 4

Preparing to conduct a parenting capacity evaluation entails a number of steps, including accepting the referral, clarifying the referral questions, determining what information should be gathered, and setting up a plan for data collection. Given the variety of settings and arrangements in which mental health practitioners operate, the psycholegal questions vary, as do expectations regarding the content and format of the evaluation report. Evaluators will be more qualified to undertake forensic mental health assessment in some cases than others. This chapter reviews potential forensic contexts and considerations in accepting the referral, framing referral questions, and developing an assessment agenda. Tips for collecting and reviewing records, a task that typically begins before the first assessment session, are described in Chapter 5.

Diversity of Forensic Contexts

Forensic assessment practices differ considerably across child protection locales and jurisdictions. MHPs may be affiliated with a private practice, a community mental health center (i.e., in a hospital or community clinic), or a court clinic. They may conduct evaluations independently or as part of a multidisciplinary assessment team (e.g., Jacobson, Miller, & Kirkwood, 1997). Methods of reimbursing evaluators vary as well (e.g., contracted clinician, case-specific fee, or salaried employee). Grisso and Quinlan (2005) surveyed professionals involved in providing court-ordered evaluations in 87 of the largest juvenile court jurisdictions nationwide. Although their survey focused on clinicians who provided delinquency evaluations, most participants reported that they also were responsible for evaluations in dependency cases. Grisso and Quinlan's survey identified a variety of locations, funding sources, and financial relationships for obtaining FMHA services in juvenile court jurisdictions.

Referral for parenting capacity evaluations may come from the court, an attorney, or a caseworker. Conceivably, a parent who is a party to the proceedings could initiate the evaluation request. When assessments are court-ordered, reports typically are entered into legal evidence and become available to all parties, whereas non–court-ordered assessments become evidence in court primarily when the evaluator's testimony is invoked. Even when the evaluation is requested by child welfare staff for service planning, it may subsequently be used in court proceedings, and thus it is treated in this volume as a forensic assessment.

In light of variations in forensic evaluation contexts, the structure and resources available also vary. Ease of access to records, office and testing space, collateral informants, technicians, or support personnel affect the scope and comprehensiveness of the evaluation. The evaluation setting may have policies regarding when and where parents are seen, methods of obtaining parent consent or notification of the evaluation, expected report formats, and other logistical aspects of the evaluation process.

In addition to local practice parameters, several general resources are available to guide the practitioner in performing FMHAs in child protection matters, as reviewed in Chapter 2. These include the American Psychological Association (APA) Ethical Principles of Psychologists and Code of Conduct (2002); the Standards for Educational and Psychological Testing (American Educational Research Association, APA & National Council on Measurement in Education, 1999); the Specialty Guidelines for Forensic Psychologists (hereafter referred to as the Specialty Guidelines— Committee on Ethical Guidelines for

INFO

Court-ordered assessments typically are entered into legal evidence and available to all parties, whereas non–court-ordered assessments typically are only introduced as evidence if the evaluator provides testimony.

Forensic Psychologists, 1991); the APA's Record Keeping Guidelines (2007), and the APA Guidelines for Psychological Evaluations in Child Protections Matters (1999) (hereinafter referred to as the APA Guidelines for Psychological Evaluations). The MHP needs to become proficient in these aspects of the assessment and resolve any ethical or logistical issues prior to beginning an assessment, so that the assessment can proceed smoothly.

Deciding Whether to Accept the Referral

Although caseworkers and lawyers often turn to MHPs to provide evaluations on parenting issues, the referring party may or may not have a realistic expectation about what a parenting assessment can provide. Table 4.1 lists some general features of what parenting assessments can and cannot do (Budd, 2005; Condie, 2003). Often, misunderstandings about what to expect from parenting assessments arise because referral sources are unfamiliar with the limitations of social science research (e.g., re: predicting individual behavior from group characteristics, making inferences from indirect indicators, predicting future behavior based on past performance, or ruling out the influence of competing variables). Explanations about the reasons for the "can'ts" listed in Table 4.1 appear throughout this volume. These guidelines may be useful in educating potential referral sources about appropriate and inappropriate referrals.

The forensic context, MHP qualifications, examinee characteristics, and presenting concerns in parenting capacity evaluations are pertinent to determining whether to accept the referral as it is articulated. Some referrals are inappropriate because they ask questions that cannot be answered using available psychological methods and known scientific bases (e.g., whether alleged but unconfirmed past abuse actually occurred, whether an abusive parent will abuse the child in the future, whether a parent or child is telling the truth—Condie, 2003). In order to maintain and use knowledge consistent with accepted clinical and scientific standards (Specialty Guidelines, 1991), the referral questions need to

Table 4.1 | What Parenting Assessments Can and Cannot Do
(reprinted with permission from Budd, 2005, p. 436)

Parenting Assessments *Can*:

- Describe characteristics and patterns of a parent's functioning in adult and childrearing roles

- Explain possible reasons for abnormal or problematic behavior, and the potential for change

- Identify person-based and environmental conditions likely to positively or negatively influence the behavior

- Describe children's functioning, needs, and risks in relation to the parent's skills and deficits

- Provide directions for intervention

Parenting Assessments *Cannot*:

- Compare an individual's parenting fitness to universal parenting standards (since none exist)

- Ascertain whether or not abuse or neglect occurred

- Determine whether a parent fits a profile of perpetrator characteristics

- Determine whether a parent or child is telling the truth

- Draw conclusions about parenting adequacy based only on indirect measures

- Predict parenting capacity from mental health diagnoses

- Rule out the effects of situational influences (e.g., time limitations, demand characteristics, current stressors, cultural issues) on the assessment process

- Predict future behavior with certainty

- Answer questions not articulated by the referral source

be revised (as described below), or the request should be turned down.

Other referrals may be inappropriate because the requested information is easily available in prior evaluations or caseworker reports. This is often the case with broad questions such as, "What is the parent's cognitive functioning?" or "What services has the parent been offered and completed?" Such questions may be posited because prior records have not been circulated, or as a substitute for case planning. On the other hand, when prior evaluations are voluminous or discrepant, a referral may be appropriate to sort out and summarize prior information in light of current functioning. A third type of inappropriate referral relates to questions that are tangential or "fishing expeditions" (Budd, 2005). Examples include referrals for evaluation of substance abuse or sexual abuse risk when there is no indication of a problem related to these issues. Whenever possible, the MHP should attempt to ascertain whether an evaluation is merited based on what is already known regarding the case. Suggestions for how to do so are discussed in the next section on framing the referral questions.

The MHP's qualifications are relevant in determining whether to accept a referral. As stated in the Specialty Guidelines (1991, p. 658), evaluators should "provide services only in areas of psychology in which they have specialized knowledge, skill, experience, and education." Beyond the provisions defined by the discipline and state regulations, the MHP needs to (1) have a background in forensic assessment concepts and methods, (2) be familiar with child protective services and local child welfare practices, and (3) possess specialized clinical skills, including cultural and linguistic competence, in assessing families involved in the child welfare system. In cases where an evaluator lacks training, plans should be made to obtain consultation, assistance, or supervision.

4
chapter

BEWARE
Do not accept any referral that:

● asks questions that cannot be answered using psychological methods or scientific bases

● asks for information that is readily available elsewhere

● asks questions about problems that are not indicated

An evaluator's competence to conduct an FMHA is likely to vary across cases. An MHP who is qualified to evaluate parenting of school-aged children or adolescents may lack the knowledge of early childhood and parent-infant attachment needed to evaluate the parenting of young children. An MHP may be knowledgeable about the assessment of parents with limited intellectual capacity but not of parents with severe mental illness. Considering the ethnic and racial diversity of the population served by CPS, evaluators need to be well versed in culturally sensitive and informed assessment procedures, including crafting recommendations that are appropriate for the individual. (Challenges and strategies related to culturally competent assessment are discussed in Chapters 3 and 5.) The circumstances of some child-maltreatment cases (e.g., severe abuse, domestic violence, or homicide) are so emotionally provocative and value-laden that an MHP may feel unable to conduct an objective evaluation. When an MHP's values preclude an objective and informed evaluation, the Specialty Guidelines (1991, p. 658) advise the MHP to decline participation or limit their involvement in a manner consistent with professional obligations (APA Ethics Code, 2002). Likewise, the APA Guidelines for Psychological Evaluations (1999) advise that evaluators in child protection cases seek consultation from experts when dealing with areas such as physical disability, sexual orientation, or other aspects of human diversity when they are outside the psychologist's scope of knowledge and competence.

In accepting a referral, the evaluator considers his relationship with the individuals to be assessed. The Specialty Guidelines (1991, p. 659) recommend

that forensic professionals "avoid providing services to parties in a legal proceeding with whom they have personal or
professional relationships that are inconsistent with the anticipated relationship."
Such a situation arises when the MHP

BEWARE
Do not
agree to financial compensation
contingent upon the outcome of
the case.

serves as both evaluator and therapist for a parent or child. If a dual
relationship cannot be avoided in regions where few qualified forensic
professionals are available, the Specialty Guidelines caution the professional to "take reasonable steps to minimize the potential negative
effects of these circumstances on the rights of the party, confidentiality, and the process of treatment and evaluation" (p. 659). The same
precaution as applied to child protection cases appears in the APA
Guidelines for Psychological Evaluations (1999).

Issues relating to financial reimbursement for an evaluation
may arise when the referral comes from a parent or an attorney
rather than through an established referral system. As a general
rule in parent-initiated cases, the MHP should make contact with
the parent's legal representative to determine if the referral is
appropriate. The Specialty Guidelines (1991, p. 658) list the fee
structure as one of the topics to be covered in the initial consultation with the legal representative of the party seeking services.
They further admonish psychologists to avoid providing services
on the basis of "contingent fees," wherein the evaluator's pay is
dependent on case outcome (p. 659).

Framing the Referral Questions

The APA Guidelines for Psychological Evaluations (1999) state
that the purposes of child protection evaluations will be determined by the nature of the child protection matter. Despite this
aspirational principle, in practice, the clarity of referral questions
and amount of background information provided varies substantially across sources. When information is inadequate, the evaluation process is not likely to proceed well. Budd and colleagues
(2001) found that most referrals for parent evaluations in the
urban child protection court system they studied failed to delineate

specific referral purposes, a factor that appeared to contribute to the limited usefulness of the resulting reports. MHPs often receive vague referral requests (e.g., "evaluate parenting ability" or "assess this father's cognitive and emotional functioning"), which must be translated into specific questions. Dyer (1999) noted that issues related to the history of the case, agency expectations, or timelines for reunification may not be conveyed to MHPs until after the report is received—too late to address or incorporate the information into the evaluation. Thus, a crucial step in preparing for the evaluation is to clarify the assessment objectives and content.

As Beyer (1993) stated, an assessment is only as useful as the questions presented to the evaluator. She recommended that the evaluator clarify (1) what, specifically, the referral source wants to know about the parent's functioning, (2) what problems or events gave rise to the concerns, and (3) what specific outcomes or options will be affected by the findings. Translating generic questions into specific referral questions often requires a dialogue about the reasons for clinical concern, the circumstances that make the questions relevant at the present time, and how the answers will be used (Budd, 2001). Potential referral questions resulting from this process could translate a generic question such as, "What is this parent's caregiving ability and what services are needed?" into the following: (1) "What strengths and weaknesses does this parent have in terms of her or his ability to adequately care for the infant and preschool-age child?" (2) "Given that the parent has a history of bipolar disorder, what, if any, mental health services are recommended?" and (3) "Are there concerns about the children's safety during visitation, and, if so, what indicators should be monitored before, during, or after visits?" Ideally the questions should be written as open-ended rather than yes/no questions.

When a referral is made with reference to a pending legal decision (such as visitation arrangements, permanency goal, or other issues), one or more questions should pertain directly to the legal decision. For example, the court may be considering a

BEST PRACTICE
Always clarify the objectives of the assessment before accepting a referral. Work with the referral source to translate generic referral requests into specific questions.

change in visitation arrangements (e.g., moving from unsupervised day visits to unsupervised overnight visits). A referral question framed to address this issue may be stated as, "What are the risk and protective factors associated with beginning unsupervised overnight visits?" When returning home is one permanency goal option currently before the court, a referral question may be, "What is the likelihood that the mother will be able to meet her child's needs if the child is returned home?"

When the state is considering termination of a parent's rights, referral questions may be framed to address the statutory criteria for termination. For example, Illinois requires a licensed clinician to assess a parent in relation to the criteria of "unfitness" listed in the Illinois Adoption Act (750 ILCS 50/1 Definitions, part D, ground P). Specifically, according to the statute, the clinician is directed to address (1) whether the parent currently has a mental impairment, mental illness, or mental retardation as defined in the state's mental health code; (2) how the parent's current condition, if any, affects his/her ability to discharge parental responsibilities; and (3) if there is evidence that the parent cannot discharge parental responsibilities due to his condition, to what extent the evidence suggests that his inability will extend beyond a reasonable time period as indicated in the Illinois Adoption Act. In some jurisdictions, attorneys may urge that the wording of referral questions subsume the language of the statute, whereas other jurisdictions have viewed expert opinions on the ultimate facts as impermissible (Condie, 2003).

Finally, when a parent is considering voluntary relinquishment of parental rights, an evaluation may be requested regarding the parent's capacity to understand and make this decision. The questions may embrace the individual's (1) ability to understand information relevant to the decision; (2) ability to appreciate the significance of the decision and its consequences; (3) ability to reason with relevant information so as to weigh all possible options; and (4) ability to express a choice that is both clear and free of duress or coercion (Baerger & Budd, 2003, p., 5).

In the urban court system studied by Budd and colleagues (2001), a comprehensive reform model was developed to address the systemic problems identified. One component of the reform model is a clinical coordination function in which master's level mental health professionals are assigned to specific courtrooms as liaisons between the court and the MHPs (Kavanaugh et al., 2006; Scally et al., 2001–2002). The clinical coordinators screen evaluation inquiries from court personnel and formalize requests for clinical information using a standard protocol called a Request for Clinical Information (RCI) form. A sample form based on the RCI form is provided in Figure 4.1. Once the RCI is completed by the clinical coordinator, it is circulated among court personnel and the

---

SAMPLE REQUEST FOR CLINICAL INFORMATION (RCI)
CHILD PROTECTION DIVISION
HALLELUYAH COUNTY COURT

If there is a signed court order, please attach it to this form.

Judge_____ Person completing form_____
Date_____

Identifying Information:

Minor_____
Subject of Request_____
Date of Birth_____
Date of Birth_____
Court#_____
Relationship to Minor_____
Caseworker_____
Agency_____
Phone#_____
Address_____

Legal Information:

Most Recent Stage of Legal Proceedings (e.g., temporary custody, adjudication, permanency hearing, termination petition filed) and Last Court Date:
_____

Next State of Legal Proceedings:
_____

Next Court Date: _____

Date Clinical Information is Needed: _____

Describe Legal History of Case (e.g., date temporary custody taken, date of adjudication and findings, date and nature of disposition):
_____
_____
_____
_____
_____

Figure 4.1 Sample Request for Clinical Information Form, adapted with permission from Cook County Juvenile Court Clinic.

Clinical Information Request:

Specify pending legal decision for which clinical information is requested (e.g., visitation, considering change of permanency goal, termination of parental rights, competence to consent of adoption, return home, case closure, no legal decision/service only):

_____
_____
_____
_____

Why is the information being requested at this time? (e.g., what events, problems, changes, or new circumstances give rise to the request now?):

_____
_____
_____
_____

Given the pending legal decision and the reason the information is being requested, what specific clinical questions would you like addressed? (e.g., what clinical information do you want to know?) List as specific questions and number each:

_____
_____
_____
_____
_____
_____

Legal Counsel:
Number: **Phone**

State's Attorney_____
Public Defender_____
Guardian AdL item_____
Attorney for CPS_____
Private Attorney_____

Figure 4.1 (Cont'd)

CPS representative to ensure that the questions meet each party's needs. The RCI differs importantly from a checklist on which the referral source simply marks boxes for topics to be evaluated. The RCI provides a structure for collecting case-specific information through a dialogue between the referral source and the mental health professional. This process, together with additional reform components, has been shown to result in substantially more specific referral questions and FMHAs that met criteria recommended in the forensic literature (Budd et al., 2006).

Although most MHPs do not have the resources of a clinical coordinator to assist in crafting specific referral questions, they may be able to implement a variation on the RCI to facilitate focused referral questions. The questions of *what* the referral source wants to know, *why* this information is requested now, and *how* the information will be used are critical to directing the evaluator toward agreed-upon assessment objectives. Direct communication not only provides the MHP with important information but also serves to educate referring parties about what can be expected from the FMHA.

Developing the Assessment Agenda

Once the referral questions are clear, they form the basis for planning the scope and direction of the evaluation (APA Guidelines for Psychological Evaluation, 1999). The MHP reviews what is known about the case, requests pertinent records for review, and develops a preliminary assessment agenda. Based on the information needed, the MHP can plan logistics such as the parties to be included in the assessment, the location and number of sessions, and potential measures and methods for data collection. The planning process allows the MHP to anticipate the need for consultation, assistance, or supervision on specialized issues outside the evaluator's areas of expertise. The assessment agenda may be revised in an iterative process as records are reviewed and the evaluation proceeds.

In the interests of efficiency and relevance, the MHP should tailor the assessment agenda to the individual case in order to investigate information not already known, corroborate pertinent details, and resolve discrepancies. For example, imagine a case in which records describe a strong positive relationship between the parent and child, but other sources suggest that the parent is inconsistent in visitation and prone to putting her own needs before the child's needs. The assessment should gather information to assess the validity of these claims and develop potential explanatory factors. The content and comprehensiveness needed in parenting capacity assessments vary from case to case. Chapter 5 describes priority topics and methods of data collection, as well as circumstances under which

BEST PRACTICE

Planning of the evaluation should begin immediately after acceptance of the referral. Begin by reviewing what is known about the case, requesting relevant records, and developing a preliminary assessment agenda.

additional methods are needed. In general, however, MHPs in child protection cases operate with limited resources, time pressures, and other practical challenges that limit the thoroughness of the evaluation.

BEST PRACTICE
Begin the parenting capacity evaluation process by assessing and organizing the individual's parenting strengths and weaknesses and related risk and protective factors.

Despite these limitations, thoughtful planning increases the likelihood that the available resources can be directed toward gathering the most pertinent information possible. The APA Guidelines for Psychological Evaluations (1999) advise MHPs to appreciate the need for timeliness in child protection matters.

Conceptualizing Parenting Strengths and Weaknesses

A central task in planning a parenting capacity evaluation is to organize what is known and not known about the parent's caregiving skills and deficits in relation to the child's functioning and needs. Several authors (e.g., Benjet, Azar, & Kuersten-Hogan, 2003; Dyer, 1999; Ostler, 2008) have noted that psychiatric diagnoses do not provide a useful means of determining parenting capacity because of the heterogeneity in the quality of parenting styles among parents with the same diagnoses. For example, some individuals with severe depression or substance abuse are unable to parent, whereas others can provide acceptable childcare except during major clinical episodes. Similarly, there is little research to support a presumption that psychiatric diagnoses predict amenability to parenting interventions or that parents remain "unfit" even when their diagnostic status changes (Benjet et al., 2003). Instead, a functional assessment model (Grisso, 1986; 2003) is recommended, as described in Chapter 2. A functional assessment focuses on what the parent knows, understands, believes, and can do regarding parenting, as well as potential variables associated with parenting skills and deficits.

Considering the lack of consensus about what constitutes minimally adequate

BEWARE
Evaluators in child protection cases have limited resources and time. Planning ahead is essential.

parenting, operational definitions of "good enough" parenting do not exist. Nevertheless, legal (Kirkland, 2003; Kreeger, 2003) and mental health (e.g., Azar, Lauretti, & Loding, 1998; Budd, 2001; Budd & Holdsworth, 1996) writers agree that evaluators should strive to apply a minimal parenting threshold in parenting capacity evaluations. As discussed in Chapter 2, minimal parenting competence has been described as "the 'floor' of acceptable parenting sufficient to protect the safety and well being of the child" (Budd, 2001, p. 3). Table 4.2 suggests areas to consider in evaluating a parent's ability to provide for a child's basic physical, cognitive/developmental, and emotional needs. The table is drawn from Budd's (2001) clinical practice model and training materials used in the Cook County Juvenile Court Clinic (CCJCC) (2008). Given the current lack of specific definitions of minimally adequate parenting, the MHP is left to make judgments about adequacy without clear markers or behavioral indicators along a continuum from optimal to inadequate parenting.

Assessing Risk and Protective Factors

Another task entailed in planning for the evaluation involves organizing what is already known about parenting strengths and weaknesses, as well as possible explanations for parenting deficiencies. In order to organize information about factors that influence parenting strengths and weaknesses, it is helpful to think in terms of risk and protective factors. CCJCC (2008) described *risk factors* as the factors that are known to be associated with or predictive of negative outcomes: that is, factors that are likely to lead to the needs of the child not being met. *Protective factors* are the factors that protect or buffer a child against negative developmental outcomes; that is, factors that are likely to lead to the needs of the child being met, or characteristics that decrease the impact of abuse or neglect. As reviewed in Chapter 3, certain child, parent, and community-level factors have been found in research to be associated with increased or decreased risk for child abuse or neglect.

Table 4.2 | Parenting to Address Child's Needs

The child's physical, cognitive, and emotional needs require minimally adequate parenting in the following areas:

● *Physical needs* (e.g., need for parenting that provides for physical safety, adequate supervision and protection from harm, a stable and safe home environment, medical and dental care, and clothing)

● Cognitive/developmental needs (e.g., need for parenting that is sensitive to the child's developmental level, has appropriate expectations for what the child can and cannot do, communicates in a developmentally appropriate and clear manner, imparts knowledge and fosters development and learning in areas of language, self-care, school functioning, and social skills)

● Emotional needs (e.g., need for parenting that reads the child's cues or moods without distortion, shows emotional affection and sensitivity, uses appropriate discipline to promote positive behavior and growth, is empathic and supportive)

Factors affecting the fit between a child's needs and a parent's caregiving capabilities include:

● The specific child's developmental stage and whether the child has any special needs or delays.

● The parent's ability to not only meet the specific child's needs (parent–child fit), but also the parent's ability to meet his or her own needs.

● The role of factors such as culture, socioeconomic status, frequency of contact with the child, and interpersonal stressors on functional parenting skills.

4
chapter

These factors provide a starting point for MHPs when assessing a parent in the context of the specific child and the environment in which the parent lives. By thinking about risks and protective factors when planning the evaluation, rather than waiting until one interprets the results, MHPs can prioritize assessment activities to further examine these factors.

Table 4.3 provides a list of risk and protective factors suggested by the research literature (CCJCC, 2008). This list should

Table 4.3 | Risk and Protective Factors (from Cook County Juvenile Court Clinic, 2008, reprinted with permission)

Risk Factors

1. Child factors
   - Premature birth, birth anomalies, low birth weight, exposure to toxins in utero
   - Difficult temperament (e.g., slow to warm up, irritable, anxious/withdrawn in early childhood)
   - Physical, cognitive or emotional disability
   - Chronic or serious illness
   - History of childhood trauma
   - Early separation from primary caregiver
   - Anti-social peer group
   - Age—younger children are at greater risk for physical abuse and neglect
   - Externalizing behavior problems (e.g., aggression, attention deficits)
   - Factors specific to sexual abuse risk: female gender, having lived without a biological father or with a stepfather, disruption of relationships with parents, maternal employment outside of the home, older age, developmental disability

2. Parental/Family factors
   - A pattern of abusive and/or neglectful behavior, prior reports of maltreatment, use of physical discipline
   - Personality characteristics (e.g., lack of trust, external locus of control, feelings of insecurity, limited capacity for empathy/guilt/remorse, self-centeredness, hostile and critical behavior, controlling tendencies, chronic irritability or negative emotional state)
   - Cognitive delays or mental retardation which could manifest in impaired judgment and problem solving skills, poor communication skills, limited parenting knowledge and skills, difficulty learning and generalizing parenting knowledge, impaired reading and comprehension
   - Psychopathology or mental illness (e.g., depression, anxiety, psychosis)
   - Exposure to cumulative trauma, especially interpersonal trauma
   - Chronic physical illness
   - Poor impulse control, history of aggression/violence, violent outbursts of temper
   - Low tolerance for stress or frustration
   - Emotional regulation difficulties
   - Social isolation, lack of support
   - Lack of involvement in community or religious activities
   - High level of stress
   - Substance abuse—risk increases if concomitant addiction and mental illness
   - Criminal behavior
   - Domestic violence, high conflict relationships, high conflict separation/divorce
   - Low level of education
   - Denial of problems (e.g., parenting, mental illness) or need for treatment

- Young age—teenage status
- Childhood history of abuse
- Insecure attachment with own parents
- Family structure—single parent with lack of support and high number of children
- Unwanted pregnancy
- Tendency to use severe physical punishment and to punish children more frequently for moral transgressions, conventional social transgressions, and noncompliance
- Poor parent–child interaction/connectedness, low parental warmth and involvement, parental alienation, rejecting attitudes, unresponsiveness to child, role reversal, scapegoating of child
- Negative attitudes and attributions about child's behaviors
- Inaccurate knowledge and expectations about child development
- Difficulty in reading and responding to children's cues
- Characteristics of non-offending parents (failure to take protective action) include: passivity, helplessness, hopelessness, passive acceptance of abuse, and collusion

3. Social/Environmental factors
- Poverty, low socioeconomic status, large family size
- Stressful life events
- Lack of access to resources and support (e.g., medical care, child care, social services)
- Unemployment
- Homelessness
- Exposure to racism/discrimination
- Poor schools
- Dangerous/violent neighborhood
- Social acceptance of violence
- Political or religious views that value non-interference in families
- A hazardous home environment (e.g., open and unscreened windows, sharp objects or toxins within reach of young children, drug paraphernalia, guns or weapons, fire hazards and uncovered electrical outlets)

4
chapter

Protective Factors

4. Child factors
- Good health and development
- Above-average intelligence
- Hobbies or interests
- Good peer relationships
- Easy temperament
- Positive disposition
- Active coping style
- Positive self-esteem
- Good social skills, ability to create supportive relationships
- Internal locus of control
- Capacity to control feelings and behavior
- External attribution of blame for the maltreatment
- Spirituality, religious involvement
- Balance between seeking help and autonomy

(Continued)

Table 4.3 | Risk and Protective Factors (from Cook County Juvenile Court Clinic, 2008, reprinted with permission) (cont'd)

5. Parent/Family factors
- Emotional stability
- Secure attachment with child, positive and warm parent-child relationship
- Ability to read a child's cues or moods without gross distortions
- Parental reconciliation with own childhood of abuse
- Awareness of the influence of own difficult childhood
- Supportive relationships in childhood
- Social support (e.g., friends, family members, extended family members, service providers)
- Household rules/structure, monitoring of the child
- Stable relationships with own parents
- Positive parental role models
- Family expectations of pro-social behavior
- High parental education
- Insight (e.g., acknowledgement of parenting problems and psychiatric symptoms, the ability to recognize the effects of prior abuse or neglect on the self)
- Help-eliciting and help-seeking behaviors, such as adherence to recommended treatment regimens
- Recognition of effects of parental mental illness on the child

6. Social/Environmental factors
- Middle to high SES status
- Access to health care and social services
- Consistent parental employment
- Adequate housing
- Family participation in a religious faith or identification with a cultural group
- Good schools
- Supportive adults outside of the family who serve as role models or mentors

be viewed as an informal guide only; it was constructed to assist clinicians in conceptualizing relevant areas of inquiry, and the validity of the list has not been assessed. Another important caveat about relying on the risk-assessment literature is that risk and protective factors are derived through *probabilistic* research. That is, the link between risk factors and abuse or neglect applies at the group level and is tenuous when applied to individuals. Thus, it has limited usefulness for forensic purposes. When conducting parenting capacity evaluations, it is important to take into consideration the individual parent–child fit (i.e., whether characteristics specific to *this* child and/or *this* parent affect the level of risk or protection). It is also important to consider *why* the factor increases risk of a negative outcome or protects against a negative outcome.

Issues in Conducting Bonding or Attachment Assessments

In some jurisdictions, *bonding or attachment assessments* are sometimes requested, particularly when children have been in foster care for extended periods of time and have difficulty relating to their biological parents. MHPs are asked to provide an evaluation of the child's relationship with the biological or foster parent, to determine the risk to the child if s/he would be returned to the biological parents. Bonding or attachment assessments raise two significant issues in a child protection context: one related to a shift in the focus of the assessment to a comparison of two or more childrearing contexts for the child (as occurs in child custody evaluations) rather than on the parent's ability to provide minimally adequate care, and the second related to the availability of validated assessment tools.

Requests for a bonding or attachment assessment are more likely under some circumstances than others. In termination-of-parental-rights cases, some parents cannot meet the casework expectations because of their failure to maintain involvement when the child is in foster care, behaving in a neglectful or psychologically harmful way during supervised visitation, or outright renouncing the wish to parent the child. In those cases, the determination to move toward termination of parental rights may be made with relatively little input from the MHP. More challenging, however, are situations in which the parents have fully cooperated and met casework expectations. When the time comes to consider returning the child, there may be concern that removing the child from his or her foster placement would cause psychological harm. In jurisdictions

4
chapter

INFO

Bonding or attachment assessments are usually requested in cases where children have been in foster care for long periods of time and have difficulty relating to their biological parents.

BEWARE
Bonding
assessments are difficult to
conduct, as there are no
validated measures for assessing
attachment in the foster care
environment.

where statutes allow termination of parental rights if it is shown that the child will be endangered or harmed by a return to the parent, in spite of the fact that the parent has been rehabilitated, MHPs may be called upon to do an attachment or bonding assessment to address how the removal from the famil-iar foster parent may affect the child.

The logic for a bonding or attachment assessment in such situations is understandable. The challenge, however, comes from the fact that validated tools for assessing attachment for children in foster care do not exist. As described in Chapter 3, Ainsworth and colleagues (Ainsworth et al., 1978) developed an assessment para-digm for infants and toddlers in a research context that involved a structured observation with the parent figure and child, the intro-duction of a stressor, and a careful assessment of whether the child appears to rely on the adult for protection. Unfortunately, the circumstances of a parent–child dyad who have not been living together falls outside the parameters of this methodology, as does assessment of a child in the temporary care of a foster parent. Furthermore, assessment of children beyond the toddler or pre-school age falls outside this methodology. Clinical versions of attachment assessment have been developed for a child protection setting (Schmidt et al. 2007), yet they have not been validated in research.

Given the absence of empirical support for bonding or attach-ment assessment in a child protection context, it may be helpful to reframe the question to focus on the psycholegal issues. These questions could include how the child's removal from the foster parents may affect the child, the strengths and limitations of the child's parents, and positive and negative factors associated with return to the child's parents (not only in terms of warmth experi-enced in each environment but also the child's sense of belonging, need to know the biological parent cares for and loves the child, need to be part of the biological extended family network, and cultural factors important to the child now or potentially as the child matures). Ultimately, the determination must be made by the court, and there are many factors that are beyond the expertise of the MHP in making that final analysis. Those include, for example, moral and values questions regarding parental rights, empirical data regarding stability of foster home placements, viability of long-term foster placement as contrasted to adoption, and the inherent unfairness of comparing what a foster family might be able to provide compared to the biological parent in the way of opportunities.

Summary

Forensic assessment practices vary considerably across child protection locales and jurisdictions. Preparing for a parenting capacity evaluation begins with ensuring that the referral questions can be addressed through available methods, the evaluator is qualified to conduct the evaluation, and no conflict exists in the evaluator's role with the family. Through communication with the referral source, referral questions need to be clarified to indicate what information is needed, why it is being requested at this time, and how it will be used. Once specific referral questions have been agreed upon, the MHP develops a preliminary assessment agenda and revises it in an iterative process as records are reviewed and the evaluation proceeds.

The central task of the MHP is to respond to the referral questions in the most productive and efficient manner feasible. Evaluators should seek information on functional parenting capabilities, using the concept (albeit vague) of *minimal parenting adequacy* as a guide. Potential strategies for organizing information include identifying parenting strengths and weaknesses specific to parent–child fit in the individual case and delineating risk and protective factors related to the parent's functioning. Cautions are offered about the use of bonding or attachment assessments, until research provides a basis for applying such a methodology to the forensic context.

Data Collection | **5**

This chapter describes the major areas of data collection in parenting capacity evaluations and relevant issues to be considered in each area. Common components in forensic mental health assessment in a child protection context include *reviewing records, interviewing examinees, interviewing collateral or third party sources, observing parents with their children,* and *conducting testing.* The first two components—review of prior records and parent interview—are essential to the FMHA, in that they provide basic factual and descriptive material. The third and fourth components—collateral interviews and parent–child observation—are highly recommended for gauging the reliability of information and broadening the sources and types of data. The fifth component—testing—is often but not always needed, and the nature and extent of the testing depends on the referral concerns and available data sources. Finally, child interviews may be a part of the FMHA when children are old enough to provide independent information and their perspective is relevant.

As in all types of forensic assessment, a common challenge is finding a balance between collecting sufficient data to inform an opinion and limiting the collection of data to what is relevant for

INFO

The following are common components in child protection evaluations:

- Reviewing records
- Interviewing examinees
- Interviewing collateral or third-party sources
- Observing parents with their children
- Conducting testing (optional)
- Interviewing the child (optional)

BEST PRACTICE
Use the following questions to guide
data collection:

1. *What?* What specific information
   will the source provide? What is
   the rationale for collecting the data,
   and is this the best source of the
   data?

2. *How?* What steps should be taken
   to gather the data? Are there any
   case-specific considerations that
   may alter the process?

3. *Why not?* Are there any reasons
   not to seek information from this
   source, or any pitfalls to be
   considered?

forming that opinion in an efficient manner. Gathering data from multiple sources and using multiple methods allows the mental health professional to compare and contrast information and draw informed conclusions. However, time and resource constraints often limit what is practical in the FMHA. Further, Heilbrun (2001) cautioned that MHPs must be selective in choosing what sources to use, noting that information with low reliability will not increase the overall accuracy of the evaluation, and may, if given much weight, decrease the reliability of the conclusions.

An initial consideration in data collection is the setting for the evaluation. MHPs should always consider the impact of the setting on the parent's comfort and on the parent's right to privacy. If MHPs interview parents outside of a controlled office or agency setting, attention should be given to ensuring that the location is private, quiet, and free of distractions. For example, if an interview is conducted in the parent's home, other family members should not be present or within hearing range, and distractions such as televisions and radios should be turned off. If unable to interview in a private, quiet, and distraction free setting, MHPs should make note of this in the report.

BEST PRACTICE
Always consider the environment in
which you are conducting the
evaluation. The location should be
private, quiet, and free of distractions.
If you are unable to interview in such a
setting, be sure to indicate this in your
report.

Review of Records

Records are a critical source of information in parenting capacity evaluations. Records can illuminate how the current situation evolved, what interventions have been offered, and if or how they have been effective, and what secondary or contextual issues may be at play. Records can also assist the evaluator in assessing behavioral patterns over time. In parenting capacity evaluations, important documents to gather and review include court records, selected child welfare agency records, service records for the parent, service records for the child, and police and legal history records. See Table 5.1 for examples of potentially relevant records in each of these categories.

Record-Gathering Steps

The first step in gathering records is to identify the relevant sources. This can be done through consultation with the court or attorneys involved in the case, the child welfare agency representative, or during initial contact with the parent. Often, records can be obtained directly from the referral source (e.g., attorney, caseworker); however, MHPs should be mindful that the referral source may not provide complete records. When gathering and reviewing records, it is important to distinguish between primary sources and secondary sources. A primary source is the entity that produces the original record, whereas a secondary source is any other entity that cites or refers to that original record. Gathering records directly from the primary source is recommended when possible.

Once the evaluator has compiled a list of sources, it is necessary to obtain appropriate authorization for the release of information. For records regarding the parent, this will involve obtaining authorization from the parent. For records regarding the child, this will require obtaining authorization from the child's legal guardian, which could be the parent, a court-appointed legal guardian, or the state. At times, a court order may be necessary: for example, if the parent refuses to provide authorization for release of information deemed potentially relevant to the evaluation. Once proper authorization has been obtained, the MHP should contact the sources to inform them of the need for records and provide them with a copy of the authorization form or court order. The form should specify exactly what types of records are requested and for what time period. It is also important for MHPs

Table 5.1 | Potentially Relevant Records in Parenting Capacity Evaluations[1]

Court records
- Orders related to child protection proceedings (e.g., temporary custody, adjudication, disposition, permanency, or protective orders)
- Motions related to child protection proceedings (e.g., change in visitation, permanency goal change/planning, and case closure)
- Reports of court appointment agencies/offices (e.g., Court Appointed Special Advocates—CASA, Mediation)
- Previous court-ordered forensic evaluations

Child welfare agency records
- Child abuse and neglect investigation notes/reports
- Risk assessments
- Social histories and assessments
- Progress reports, service plans, case reviews
- Visitation logs/records
- Unusual incident reports

Service records for the parent(s)
- Psychiatric, psychological, clinical, and forensic evaluations
- Therapy and psychiatric notes, progress reports, transfer summaries, discharge summaries (inpatient and outpatient)
- Substance-abuse service records
- Domestic-violence service records
- Parenting service records and evaluations
- Academic records, including any evaluations and special-education documents
- Medical records

Service records for the child(ren)
- Psychiatric, psychological, and clinical evaluations
- Therapy and psychiatric notes, progress reports, transfer summaries, discharge summaries (inpatient and outpatient)
- Academic records, including any evaluations and special-education documents
- Medical records, including those related to allegations or findings of abuse/neglect

Police/legal history records
- Incarceration records
- Criminal history report
- Police/arrest reports

[1] This list is not exhaustive. In addition, different jurisdictions may use other terminology to refer to these types of records.

to keep detailed records of the data-gathering process (e.g., dates authorizations were sent and other efforts made to collect records, dates records were received, and number of pages provided).

Not all records generated on a case may be useful in the evaluation process. For example, casework agency records typically include documents (e.g., financial tracking forms) that will have no bearing on the referral issues and will not need to be sought, or, if received, reviewed. There are also some service records that MHPs will be able to determine are not relevant. For example, if the referral concerns relate to the history of abuse and the parent's progress in treatment, seeking complete medical records on a parent will probably be inefficient in terms of record gathering and record reviewing, because those records are likely to contain much medical information that has little or nothing to do with abuse or treatment. However, the evaluator may not be able to discern during the record-gathering process what may or may not be relevant. It is wise to only exclude the records from the gathering process that one can be confident will contain no relevant information.

Potential Challenges

There are multiple obstacles commonly encountered in gathering records, which include agency closure, unreachable or uncooperative sources, and incomplete or illegible records. In these situations, there may be little MHPs can do beyond noting in the report the obstacle to obtaining records and all attempts MHPs have made to obtain the records. Some sources require payment for records; the issue of payment may need to be resolved with the referring source. Particularly for evaluators working independently of a clinic or support

5
chapter

BEWARE When review ing records from other professionals, be careful not to be influenced by their conclusions.

staff, gathering records can be extremely time-consuming, a factor that should be considered when planning the evaluation. In the event that one is unable to obtain requested records, one should attempt to gather the information from other sources, such as collateral contacts.

As with any data source, records may be inaccurate or biased, and any conclusions drawn from them should be substantiated with information from other sources. When reviewing records that contain clinical opinions, evaluators should be careful not to interpret the author's opinions as if they were fact. Heilbrun, Warren, and Picarello (2003) noted that records from professionals may offer conclusions regarding the same areas being currently assessed. These authors caution that the MHP should "not be overly influenced by conclusions drawn by other professionals" (p. 80). Instead, they become topics for the MHP to examine for corroborating or disconfirming information as part of the current assessment.

Interviews with Examinees

Interviews with the parent are a vital part of parenting capacity evaluations. The Specialty Guidelines for Forensic Psychologists (Committee on Ethical Guidelines for Forensic Psychologists, 1991) emphasize that "forensic psychologists avoid giving written or oral evidence about the psychological characteristics of particular individuals when they have not had an opportunity to conduct an examination of the individual adequate to the scope of the statements, opinions, or conclusions" (p. 663). It is true that parents will sometimes attempt to portray themselves in the most favorable light possible, often denying their faults, minimizing responsibility for or severity of past mistakes, and presenting misinformation. Therefore, relying on parent self-report as the primary source of information may lead the evaluator to draw inaccurate conclusions. Nonetheless, this is not a reason to avoid interviews with parents. They are essential to gathering pertinent information about the parent as well as providing an opportunity to interact with and observe the parent's mental state and behaviors.

Through the course of interviews with the parent, the evaluator should gather relevant historical and current information about functioning in a variety of areas. Table 5.2 outlines potential topic areas and details specific areas of inquiry in each.

BEWARE Parents are likely to downplay faults and present misinformation in an effort to portray themselves favorably during the interview. Do not rely on parent self-report as the primary source of information.

Behavioral Observations

As part of the interview process, the evaluator should conduct a general mental status examination and make note of any relevant behavioral observations. Areas to focus on include general physical presentation; orientation to person, place, time, and situation; the presence of any delusions or symptoms of a thought disorder; memory, concentration, and attention; suicidal or homicidal thoughts; the presence of any signs of depression or mania; general mood and affect; insight and judgment; and level of cooperativeness. Also critical to assess during interviews is the parent's reliability as an informant and any factors that may limit the MHP's ability to generalize from the information collected (e.g., the parent's comprehension of questions, cognitive limitations, or distorted thinking; time limitations; and parent or child illness during sessions).

Some parent interviews may present challenges, and it is advisable to plan ahead when this can be anticipated and make adjustments as necessary. Parent factors that may lead MHPs to alter their interviewing style and manner of asking questions include cognitive limitations or mental illness, a known history of violent or unpredictable behavior, and physical disabilities. Alterations evaluators may make include simplifying language if interviewing a parent with cognitive limitations, or taking breaks if interviewing a parent who is upset or fatigued. When an evaluator is aware that a risk of violence exists, steps should be taken to assure the evaluator's safety: for example, by having a colleague present.

5 chapter

Table 5.2	Potential Content Areas for Interviewing Parents (from Cook County Juvenile Court Clinic, 2008, adapted from Budd, 2001)

Parent's family of origin
- Makeup of family (e.g., who was in the home when growing up, significant attachment figures, presence or absence of parents/attachment figures)
- Early health and development
- Childrearing and disciplinary experiences growing up (e.g., forms of discipline experienced, parent's perception of forms of discipline)
- History of family violence, substance abuse, and criminal activity
- History of abuse/maltreatment (e.g., neglect, physical abuse, sexual abuse, emotional abuse, exposure to violence and/or substance abuse, exposure to adult sexual activity)
- Continuity or discontinuity of relationships with family members and attachment figures, and why

Personal background
- Educational history
- Employment history, including reasons for jobs ending, and current status
- Medical history and current health status
- Residential history and current living situation (e.g., stability, ever homeless, nature of current home and neighborhood, people currently in household)
- Cultural and religious identity, and role this plays in day-to-day life
- Relationship history (e.g., significant-partner relationships and breakups, relationships with father of child, domestic violence in relationships, substance use of partners, criminal history of partners, current relationship status and nature/quality of relationship, involvement of current partner in childrearing, partner's childrearing views and practices)
- Legal/criminal history (e.g., arrests, convictions)

Current supports and coping skills
- Level and causes of stress in life and in parenting role
- Ways of coping with stress
- Perceived and provided sources of support (e.g., friends, family members, religious community, neighbors)
- Nature of support offered by people (e.g., emotional, informational, social, financial, instrumental)
- Frequency of contact with support network

Mental health history and current functioning
- History of mental health symptoms (e.g., nature of symptoms, onset, duration, frequency) and current functioning
- History of mental health treatment/services (e.g., outpatient treatment, inpatient treatment, psychiatric treatment/medication monitoring)
- View of past and present treatment and level of participation in treatment
- Insight into mental illness/condition and impact on functioning and parenting

Substance-abuse history and current functioning
- History of substance use (e.g., age started, types used, frequency, and duration of use)
- Triggers for substance abuse
- Treatment received for substance abuse
- View of past and present treatment and level of participation in treatment
- Insight into substance-abuse history and impact on functioning and parenting

CPS and juvenile/family court history
- Parent's version of events that brought case into system
- Parent's view of validity of concerns and personal responsibility for events
- Insight into how the events have affected the children
- View of how events have affected his/her own life
- View of relationship with CPS and court and treatment within those systems
- Services recommended and received to address parenting concerns
- Level of participation in past and present services
- View of past and present services (e.g., helpful and why, unhelpful and why)
- Hardships encountered in trying to utilize services
- Understanding of why the court is asking the current legal question and understanding of the current concerns held by the court and CPS

Parenting history and abilities
- First experiences as a parent and time spent as caregiver
- Pre- and postnatal history of children
- Early development and health of children
- Individual characteristics of children (e.g., developmental stage and abilities; emotional, behavioral, and academic functioning; temperament/personality; special needs and service needs; concerns about current and/or future well-being of children)
- Understanding of needs and developmental stages of children
- Perception of strengths and weaknesses as a parent
- View of quality of past and current relationship with children
- Current visitation schedule and contact, if children are not in parent's custody
- Things the parent would like to do for the children and ability to provide these things
- Approach to and beliefs about discipline (e.g., methods, consistency of methods used, belief about effectiveness, belief about impact on children, view of developmentally appropriate discipline, expectations of children's behaviors/compliance with rules)
- Favorite and most difficult times with children and/or in parenting role

5
chapter

Desires for and view of the future
- What would the parent like to see happen?
- What would be best for the children?
- What would the children like to have happen?
- What services or changes are needed to help the parent achieve desired outcomes?
- Willingness to engage in necessary services?
- Barriers to achieving desired outcomes?
- What would happen if desired outcomes were not achieved?

BEST PRACTICE

Always take into consideration the following when conducting a parent interview:

● Mental illness or cognitive limitations

● History of violent or unpredictable behavior

● Physical disabilities

It may be necessary to alter your interviewing style and manner of asking questions.

When unable to do so, evaluators should consider postponing the interview until appropriate precautions can be put in place. Evaluators should also be prepared to terminate an interview if at any time the parent exhibits threatening behavior.

Value of Multiple Interviews

Ideally, the FMHA will include more than one interview with a parent, although there are situations in which this is not possible. Having multiple interviews allows for a more thorough view of a parent's functioning and a better sense of the consistency and validity of the parent's responses. Multiple interviews provide a parent with time to reflect on the evaluator's questions so that the parent, probably somewhat anxious at the first interview, can provide clarification if needed. A parent may present in a very favorable light during an initial contact but be unable to sustain that presentation over multiple interviews. Finally, having multiple interviews allows the evaluator to follow up on information gleaned from records, testing, collateral contacts, and parent–child observations, and allows the parent to expand on responses or provide explanations that might not have occurred to the parent during the critical first interview. In the event that conducting a single interview is the only option, MHPs should make sure the interview is thorough and focused enough to gather essential information so the referral questions can be addressed.

Clarifying Purpose and Limits of Confidentiality

Critical issues that the evaluator should address with a parent at the start of the interviewing process include the identity and role of the MHP; the referral source and purpose of the evaluation; the limits of confidentiality, including mandated reporting issues; and the steps in the evaluation process and expectations for the parent's role. Reviewing these points verbally as well as in writing is recommended.

When discussing the purpose of the evaluation, it is important to state if the referral questions are linked to a specific legal decision to be made. For example, if the results of the evaluation will assist the court in determining if the parent's rights as a parent will be terminated, the evaluator will need to not only explain what termination of parental rights means, but also tell the parent that the information gathered for this evaluation will be used by the court to make that decision.

When outlining the limits of confidentiality, several factors need to be articulated to the parent. Key points are listed in the adjacent Best Practice Box.

Unless the parent is court-ordered to participate in the evaluation, it is necessary to obtain the parent's *informed consent* to participate *prior* to proceeding with the evaluation. After the purpose of the evaluation and limits of confidentiality are explained, the evaluator should take stock of the parent's consent to proceed or not to proceed. If the parent is unable or unwilling to provide such consent, the MHP should take steps to have the parent consult with his or her attorney regarding issues of participation (Committee on Ethical Guidelines, 1991). In the event that a parent is court-ordered to participate in the evaluation, the parent's participation is not voluntary, and therefore the parent cannot decline to consent

BEST PRACTICE

Be sure to convey the following points when discussing confidentiality with a parent:

- Nothing the parent reports to you or that you observe will be kept private or confidential.

- Anything the parent reports can be included in the report.

- The report will be provided to the referral source (and potentially to others, who should be identified).

- As the evaluator, you may also have to provide oral testimony about what the parent reports.

- If concerns arise about risk of harm to self or others, you are mandated to report this information.

- If another parent is involved in court proceedings, he or she may have access to the information provided.

5 chapter

to participate (Heilbrun, 2001). However, it still remains important to explain that the parent can refuse to participate in the evaluation or can decide to refrain from answering specific questions if he or she chooses, but that this information will be communicated to the court nonetheless.

When assessing a parent's understanding of the purpose of the evaluation, limits of confidentiality, and, as applicable, informed consent, it is important to have the parent state in his or her own words an understanding of the critical points. If a parent has difficulty understanding these issues, MHPs should spend time explaining them again and should ask open-ended questions to assess the parent's understanding. Be sure to document in the report the steps taken to ensure that the parent understood. In subsequent interviews, review these issues again to assure the parent's retention of understanding. Connell (2006) pointed out that MHPs may need to review explanations of the notice again during an interview session if a parent communicates a misunderstanding of the process. Examples include a parent who asks that something be "off the record" or who communicates that the interview sessions have been helpful, which might indicate that the parent views the evaluator in a therapeutic role.

It is not uncommon or unexpected for a parent to resist the evaluation process, given the significance of the evaluation's outcome. This resistance may be expressed through refusal to cooperate, hostility, guardedness, or apprehensiveness. Each of these presentations can lead to challenges for MHPs in gathering data. Providing the parent with as much information as possible at the start of the interview may also serve to alleviate some of the parent's resistance.

Developing and Maintaining Rapport

When developing rapport with the parent, MHPs should be aware of the difference between the role of a therapist and that of a forensic evaluator. Therapeutic rapport is characterized by a sense of trust and an alliance between therapist and client. Communication by a therapist is empathic, nonjudgmental, and affirming. Forensic evaluators, while needing to establish a cooperative working relationship so a comprehensive evaluation can be conducted, must nevertheless be careful to maintain appropriate professional reserve with the parent. MHPs must recognize that their role is not one of therapist or advocate, but rather of impartial gatherer of information to assist the legal decision-maker (Melton et al., 2007). This is not to say that MHPs should not be attentive and courteous; rather, when displaying such characteristics, it is important not to cross a line toward being therapeutic, thus misleading the parent to perceive the MHP as a helping advocate. In fact, in the context of a forensic examination, it may not be in the parent's best interest to trust the evaluator. MHPs should take into consideration cultural issues (e.g., race, ethnicity, gender, sexuality) that could play a role in establishing a cooperative working relationship and effective communication with a parent. Having sensitivity to such issues as well as insight into one's own potential for bias and reactivity to cultural issues is critical to conducting an accurate evaluation.

BEST PRACTICE
Always take into consideration any cultural issues that could affect your attempt to establish a cooperative working relationship and effective communication with the parent you are evaluating.

5
chapter

Potential Challenges

During the course of the evaluation, it is not uncommon for parents to pose some challenging questions, for which one should be prepared. Some examples might include: "What are you going to say in your report?" or "How do you think I am doing?" An appropriate response to such inquiry is to let the

BEWARE
Your role as the evaluator is to obtain information that will assist the trier of fact, not to serve as therapist or advocate for the parent. It is important that you maintain a professional and reserved manner during the evaluation.

parent know that you will not form conclusions until you have completed your data gathering and that you will explain those findings and conclusions by submitting a report to the referral source. It would also be acceptable to thank the parent for being cooperative and to acknowledge that the evaluation is a stressful process. Sometimes parents bristle at the questions posed by the evaluator regarding sensitive and personal topics in the parent's history (e.g., relationship history, childhood history of abuse), express frustration, or ask why the evaluator needs to know this information. In response, the MHP might explain the purpose of gathering a history to fully understand the parent's current functioning and to answer the referral source's questions. For example, the evaluator might state, "I realize that I am asking some very personal questions and that it is difficult to answer them. But in order to complete my evaluation, I need to have information about all areas of your life that might have influenced your own development up to now, and that could affect your parenting." If the parent continues to question the importance of the information being requested, which is not uncommon, the MHP should try to help the parent understand the connection between the topics being discussed and parenting. It is important to do so, however, without providing the parent with information that may then influence his or her answers.

Inconsistencies between parent self-report and information gathered from other sources are often encountered in parenting capacity evaluations. When faced with this, the evaluator should ask the parent in a non-accusatory, information-gathering style to address the inconsistencies. Doing so early in the evaluation process, rather than at the end, may result in the parent's using less denial overall. Melton and colleagues (2007) noted that "if such a confrontation is handled tactfully and empathically, the clinician may now have a relieved, cooperative, and candid respondent for any remaining issues to be explored" (p. 58).

MHPs may encounter constraints in getting interviews

BEST PRACTICE
Address inconsistencies between what the parent tells you and what you have gathered from other sources early in the evaluation process.

scheduled and completed (e.g., due to a rural setting, parent's lack of phone, transient/homeless status of the parent, or language barriers). When such circumstances arise, MHPs should be sure to document the

BEST PRACTICE

If you do not speak the parent's primary language, enlist the help of a certified interpreter. Do not use friends or family members of the parent, as this raises the potential for bias.

steps taken to address these issues in their notes and the report. Evaluators also should document how these factors may have affected the data collection process.

Use of interpreters when the MHP does not speak the primary language of the parent presents serious challenges in conducting a thorough evaluation. For instance, this may lead to misinterpretation of statements by the evaluator, interpreter, or parent, and may influence the relationship development and data quality overall (Azar & Benjet, 1994). When an interpreter is introduced into the interview, "the relationship is no longer a dyadic one, but is influenced by the relationships among the interpreter, the professional, and the parent" (Azar & Benjet, 1994, p. 255). If an interpreter must be used, the evaluator should seek out a certified interpreter, thereby assuring fluency and professionalism. Using a friend, child, or other family member raises the potential for bias in the interpretation due to the individual's relationship with the examinee. When using an interpreter, the MHP should also acknowledge potential limitations of the data in the report.

Two-Parent Assessments

When a referral for a parenting capacity evaluation involves two parents, there are additional factors that MHPs should take into consideration in conducting interviews. First, MHPs should be sure when reviewing the limits of confidentiality that each parent is aware the other parent may be privy to information contained in the evaluation. This may be relevant when there is sensitive information that one parent does not want his or her partner to be aware was discussed (e.g., domestic violence or extramarital sexual activity). Second, conducting both separate and joint interviews may be helpful in order to observe the parents' interactions as well as to gather information they elect to provide individually and as a couple. If one parent in an evaluation is acting as his or her own attorney (i.e., is *pro se*), particular care must be taken with the information gathered. The *pro se* parent's access to the report should be taken into consideration when deciding when and how to release the reports to the relevant parties. Ultimately, in cases that proceed to trial, parents may have access to each other's reports. Whether this is so or not, under all circumstances the evaluator should avoid creating unnecessarily dangerous or embarrassing exposure of a parent's disclosures or evaluation results. It may be helpful to ask for direction from the court regarding provision of reports to the parents, or at least to discuss this issue with both parents before the time to release the report.

Child Interviews

Although not a standard part of parenting capacity evaluations, child interviews may be relevant in certain cases. When deciding whether to conduct a child interview, MHPs should first consider the referral questions and whether direct information from the child is pertinent. Often information can be obtained from other sources, such as records or collateral interviews. Second, MHPs should consider the age and developmental level of the child, and whether the child is likely to be able to provide relevant and independent information during an interview. Third, MHPs should take into consideration the emotional functioning of the child and whether being interviewed will cause the child distress. If a MHP has concern about the emotional ramifications of conducting an interview, information may be sought from other professionals with whom the child has contact, such as caseworkers, therapists, or school personnel. Finally, MHPs may want to consider conducting an interview with a child if there is reason to believe that other available information about the child is biased or inaccurate. If a child interview is conducted, MHPs should always review the limits of confidentiality with the child.

Collateral/Third Party Interviews[1]

Gathering information from collateral sources is another important step in conducting parenting capacity evaluations. Information from collateral sources can provide another perspective on the parent and the case, thus increasing the likelihood that credible and sound conclusions will be drawn in the FMHA. Information from these sources can also assist in assessing the veracity of information provided by the parent, by offering confirmation and/or refutation of reports made. Heilbrun and colleagues (2003) noted, "One of the most important reasons to obtain [collateral information] involves the need to verify the accuracy of symptoms and behavior reported by the individual being evaluated" (p. 78). Common collateral sources include caseworkers or agency representatives, service providers, foster parents, sources of data or support named by the parent, attorneys or referral sources, and family members of the parent.

The nature of the information gathered will depend in part on the information needed to complete a thorough assessment. It also will depend on what information the source is capable of providing and how reliable the source is assessed to be. Heilbrun and colleagues (2003) described problems that can limit the accuracy of collateral information, including reluctance to participate, bias, lack of specific expertise, suggestibility, and memory loss. They suggested reviewing all available documents prior to interviewing

---

1   These terms are used interchangeably in the field; for this chapter, the term *collateral* is
     used.

BEST PRACTICE
When interviewing collateral sources, ask only about areas for which you have reason to believe the source can provide reliable and unbiased information.

collateral sources in order to be able to ask informed questions, provide non-confidential details to the interviewee that he or she may not recall, and clarify if inconsistent information is provided by the interviewee.

It is important to inquire about information only within the scope of what the collateral source is able to provide. For example, if interviewing the parent's therapist, inquiring about the functioning of the child may yield inaccurate information. Likewise, asking the parent's individual therapist his or her opinion on that person's parenting skills will be of limited value if the therapist has never seen the parent with the child. It is important to inquire only about areas for which there is reason to believe the source can provide reliable and unbiased information. For example, if one is interviewing a foster parent, relevant areas of inquiry may include the foster child's emotional and behavioral functioning, but not the foster parent's opinion on the birth parent's caregiving skills or relationship with the child. Likewise, if assessing a parent's current mental state, interviewing a psychiatrist who treated the parent five years ago might not be a useful step.

Parent–Child Observations

Parent–child observations are a valuable component of parenting capacity evaluations and should be conducted whenever feasible, unless contraindicated by the circumstances of the case. Observations should be avoided, for example, in cases of physical abuse when contact with the parent perpetrator may be traumatizing or otherwise harmful to the child. Unlike child interviews, parent–child observations do not depend on the child's developmental or emotional capacity in order to be useful. Observing a parent in interactions with the child provides concrete information about the parent's caregiving strengths and weaknesses, ability to meet the child's individual needs, and the nature of the parent–child relationship. Observations can also provide important information about the general functioning (e.g., emotional, behavioral, social) of the parent and child. Although in this chapter reference is made to observing the "child," it is recommended that MHPs observe parent-child interactions with all children in the parent's care who are relevant to the reason for referral. Table 5.3 outlines areas MHPs should attend to when observing parents and children interact. Observation of the safety of the home environment, if not already reported on by other sources (e.g., a caseworker), may also be necessary.

Choosing a Location

Ideally, parent–child observations will occur in a natural setting (American Psychological Association Committee on Professional Practice and Standards, 1999)—that is, a setting in which the parent and child are used to interacting. This allows for the parent and child to feel most at ease and comfortable. For example, if interactions between the parent and child typically occur in the parent's home, or the child resides with the parent, conducting the observation in that setting will provide the most valuable and real-istic information. If visitation occurs at an agency, this setting could be used for observation. MHPs may also have occasion to observe a parent and child interact in the office waiting area; it is critical, however, that the parent has been fairly warned that this interaction is being observed as part of the examination process.

Observation of the child in the foster home typically is not called for and may introduce complications that can confound the objectivity of the parenting capacity evaluation. The principal risk is that the MHP may lose sight of the primary purpose of the evaluation, which is to assess the examinee's parenting strengths and weaknesses and the parent–child relationship. Observing the child in the foster home may lead to a subtle shift toward com-parison of the parent with the foster parent and the foster parent's relationship with the child. Unlike a custody evaluation, the purpose of the FMHA in child protection is not to compare two parenting environments,

BEST PRACTICE
Conduct parent–child observations in settings that are familiar to the parent and child.

5
chapter

Table 5.3 | Observation Areas for Parent–Child Interactions (drawn from Azar, Lauretti, & Loding, 1998; Budd, 2001; Cook County Juvenile Court Clinic, 2008; Hynan, 2003; Pezzot-Pearce & Pearce, 2004)

Parent's general mental state and behaviors in relation to the child
- Are there indications of stability or of impairment in overall functioning (e.g., signs of mental illness, cognitive impairment, being under the influence of a substance)?
- Is the parent engaged and present in the interaction with the child, or does the parent appear distracted, bored, or withdrawn?

Parent's ability to provide structure and safety
- How does the parent structure interactions?
- Does the parent set appropriate rules and limits, and is the parent able to enforce and follow through with such limits?
- Does the parent foster an environment in which the child is physically safe?
- Is the parent aware of and responsive to the child's basic physical needs (e.g., hunger, need to use the bathroom, safety concerns)?
- How does the parent make the child aware of misbehavior, and does the parent correct such behavior in a constructive way?

Parent's ability to foster growth and development
- Does the parent communicate effectively and in an age-appropriate manner with the child?
- Does the parent display understanding or misunderstanding of the child's developmental level (e.g., allowing child the opportunity for exploration and autonomy, providing age-appropriate affection)?
- How does the parent display acceptance or disapproval of the child's behavior?
- Does the parent encourage or reinforce negative behavior from the child?
- Does the parent encourage or reinforce positive behavior from the child?
- Does the parent make efforts to teach the child new skills, and, if so, does the parent do so effectively?
- Is the parent able to communicate expectations in a clear and appropriate manner?
- Is the parent able to accept the child's right to disagree or hold a different opinion?

Parent's ability to provide nurturance, acceptance, and empathy
- Is the parent able to provide sufficient attention to more than one child at a time?
- Is the parent able to express and/or display positive and warm feelings toward the child?
- Is the parent able to be appropriately responsive to and aware of the child's feelings and special needs?
- Is the parent able to balance his or her own needs and feelings with those of the child?

- Is the parent able to accurately read and be responsive to the child's cues (e.g., appropriately reads facial expressions and body language, expresses attention/affection, responds to signs of distress, responds positively to child's attempts to initiate communication)?
- Does the parent discuss inappropriate topics with the child or make concerning comments (e.g., comment negatively about the other parent or the caseworker, swear, inappropriately tease, adopt a hostile tone, discuss age-inappropriate topics?)

Child's general mental state and behavior
- What is the temperament of the child?
- Does the child display behavioral or emotional problems?
- Is the child functioning at a developmentally appropriate level, or does the child display developmental impairment?

Child's behaviors in relation to the parent
- Is the child at ease around and interested in the parent?
- Does the child initiate interactions with the parent?
- Does the child display behavioral or emotional difficulties that challenge the parent's response strategies?
- Does the child appear comfortable with disagreeing with the parent and talking about a range of topics?
- How does the child show affection or interest in the parent?

but rather to inform the court on issues related to whether the parent who is the subject of the evaluation is able to provide minimally adequate parenting. (The rationale and basis for this guiding premise is discussed in Chapter 2.)

There may, however, be cases when the purpose of the evaluation is to assess the child's behavior and functioning in different contexts and the probable impact of a move from foster care. Schmidt and colleagues (2007) noted that observing the child in the foster home provides "a means of comparing the child with different caregivers and to understand if the child's response and interaction with his/her parent is unique or a general pattern of behavior" (p. 255). In such circumstances, one must recognize clearly that the purpose is not to assess the parenting skills of the foster parent, but rather to gather information about the child's functioning in that caregiving context.

BEWARE Observing the child in the foster home environment can lead to comparison of the parent and foster parent, which is not relevant to the assessment.

In general, whether observing the child with the parent or with other caregivers, the MHP must be cautious about drawing conclusions based on that observation. The child's behavior may be attributable to any one of a host of factors beyond those related to parenting. The child may act out with one caregiver, for example, because of distress about having just been separated from another caregiver. Or the child may be clingy and fussy during an observation because the child has just awakened from a nap or is developing a cold. The child may lash out angrily at a parent during an observed visit because of fear based on prior negative interactions with the parent, because the child is angry about being apart from the parent, or because of an immediately preceding event (such as needing to stop playing) unrelated to the interaction. When sampling the child's behaviors, it is tempting to attribute causation in a way that confirms one's working hypotheses (of either a positive or negative sort), when the focus should be, instead, on how the parent manages the child's behavior or what level of insight the parent displays about the child's needs and capacities.

Structuring the Observation

In conducting parent–child observations, it is useful to have both unstructured and structured interactions between the parent and child (Azar et al., 1998; Schmidt et al., 2007; Wilson et al., 2008). Wilson and colleagues (2008) noted that "unstructured activities may allow for a greater observable range of parental involvement" (p. 910) than structured activities alone. When initiating structured time, it is important to provide activities that will yield information relevant to the developmental age of the child and the parent's ability to interact with the child in a developmentally appropriate manner. For example, when observing a parent with an infant, the MHP could request that the parent change a diaper or feed the baby. When observing a parent with a toddler or preschooler, the MHP could ask the parent to read the child a story, play a game with the child, or instruct the child to clean up the toys. When observing a parent with a school-age child or teenager, the MHP could ask the parent to help the child with schoolwork

or engage the child in a dialogue
about a specific topic. Another
way to include structured time is
to schedule the observation at a
time when the MHP can observe
mealtimes, bedtime routines, or

BEST PRACTICE
Be sure to include both structured and
unstructured activities during parent–
child observations.

bathing (Schmidt et al., 2007). When choosing activities, it is also
useful to assign the parent a moderately stressful task during the
observation so the evaluator can observe the parent's ability to
respond to the child's distress and to manage his or her own stress
(Azar et al., 1998; Schmidt et al., 2007).

Some structured observation tools have been designed for use
during parent–child observations. These include the Dyadic
Parent–Child Interaction Coding System (DPICS) (Eyberg et al.,
2005) and the Home Observation for the Measurement of the
Environment (HOME) Inventory (Caldwell & Bradley, 1984).
However, the applicability of these tools in parenting capacity
evaluations has not been studied. The strengths as well as the
limitations of standardized observational measures are discussed in
Chapter 3. Furthermore, Budd (2001), in her discussion of parent–child observation tools, noted that, due to the "individualized
circumstances giving rise to parental fitness assessments, it often is
not feasible to employ standardized observation formats" (p. 12).
For example, the DPICS structures the observation of a parent and
one child between the ages of two and seven years, and it entails
three structured situations over a 25-minute period. It is difficult
to compare data obtained from the DPICS in standard cases to
those with parent–child sessions involving more than one child or
children not in this age range. Furthermore, these structured
observational tools were designed for use in research and intervention programs, so their relevance and reliability in assessing parenting in the specialized circumstances of child-protection evaluations
are unstudied. A further limitation of such measures is the extensive training required for proper administration and coding.

The forensic assessment literature has not outlined clear guidelines for the number of observations that should be included in a
parenting capacity evaluation. However, the literature has suggested

5
chapter

increased validity of conclusions when they are drawn from more than one observation, for longer periods of time, and from observations conducted in different settings. Azar et al. (1998) proposed that "data aggregated over a number of sessions may have greater stability and thus may provide a more accurate assessment of typical interactions" (p. 87). Similarly, Schmidt et al. (2007) noted that repeated observations give "further validity to any patterns of interaction observed" (p. 255). Although ideally MHPs will conduct multiple parent–child observations, potentially in different settings, it is often difficult to do so. As to the length of observations, longer observations (i.e., more than 60 minutes) have been found to yield observable differences in behavior displayed by maltreating as compared to non-maltreating parents (Wilson et al., 2008). Moreover, longer observations not only allow the parent and child to engage in more interaction, but they also provide greater potential for the parent to experience potential stress or difficult situations within the parenting role (Schmidt et al., 2007; Wilson et al., 2008).

MHPs should be aware of ways in which the conditions of parent–child observations can sometimes produce data that are difficult to interpret. A parent may interact with a child in an atypically positive manner due to attempts to put forth the best behavior or due to awareness of being observed. An observation of short duration may also lead the evaluator to observe an unrealistic portrayal of skills. Although awareness of and anxiety about the weight of the examination may lead a parent to perform well during an observation, such factors may also lead a parent to display atypically negative behaviors. Observations also may be affected by recent lack of contact between the parent and child, which could result in the visit's appearing awkward or uncomfortable for the parent and/or child. It may be useful to ask parents how the observation was similar or different from their usual time with their child.

INFO

Although there are no clear guidelines regarding the optimal number and length of parent–child observations, it has been suggested that multiple observations, conducted for longer periods of time and in varying settings, lead to more valid conclusions.

It may not always be clinically sound to conduct a parent–child observation. For instance, if a parent and child have not had any contact in the recent past, behaviors observed may not accurately reflect the parent–child dynamic. If contact has been limited due to safety con-

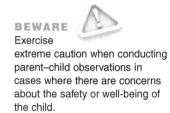

BEWARE Exercise extreme caution when conducting parent–child observations in cases where there are concerns about the safety or well-being of the child.

cerns (e.g., violent or erratic behavior from the parent) or concerns about the well-being of the child (e.g., emotionally unstable behavior from the parent), MHPs should be extremely cautious about conducting an observation. There may also be times when a child expresses a desire to not have contact with the parent. In such situations the evaluator should consider the reasons for the child's statements, the independence of the child's feelings about contact, and the developmental age of the child before proceeding. There may also be legal and physical barriers to conducting observations, such as a court order prohibiting contact between the parent and child, incarceration of a parent, and geographical distance between parent and child. In these situations, gathering information from a collateral source may provide useful information. When the safety and well-being of the child are not at issue, MHPs should make all attempts to overcome such barriers.

Testing

Different terms are often used to describe psychological tests, such as *measures, instruments, indexes, scales,* and *inventories.* The term *tests* will be used throughout this chapter for consistency. Although tests are often considered the exclusive province of professionals in clinical and other applied-psychology specialties, their use in forensic assessment is more circumscribed than in clinical and educational contexts. Use of psychological tests is not always necessary in parenting capacity evaluations; MHPs should beware of reflexively conducting testing or administering a standard battery of tests. When assessing the need to use psychological tests, MHPs should consider the following factors: (1) Will the test provide relevant information that cannot be obtained through other means

(e.g., review of records, clinical, or collateral interviews)? (2) Will the test provide valuable concurrent data on relevant constructs? (3) Is there evidence that the test is valid and reliable for its intended use? (4) Is there evidence regarding use of the instrument with the examinee's demographic, cultural, or ethnic group? Affirmative answers to these questions would strengthen the rationale for inclusion of a test in the assessment. MHPs should also take into consideration that testing can be costly, time consuming, and taxing for the parent. Even though conducting testing may be easier for and more familiar to MHPs than other methods of data collection, tests should be administered only when merited by the referral questions and likely to add credible information.

Common tests used in parenting capacity evaluations fall into two of the three categories described by Heilbrun, Rogers, and Otto (2002): clinical assessment measures (or traditional psychological tests) and forensically relevant instruments (or tests of specific parenting knowledge, beliefs, and perceptions). No parenting tests have been validated yet for the third category, forensic assessment measures. The choice of measures discussed in this chapter was based on the limited research base reviewed in Chapter 3 regarding assessment measures used in forensic practice. Given the dearth of research on the validity of tests with parents in a child-protection context, tests reported in forensic assessment reviews as popular and generally acceptable are discussed as well.

Traditional Psychological Tests

The constructs assessed by traditional psychological tests may only indirectly relate to parenting capacity, hence limiting their usefulness, particularly for describing parenting capabilities and deficits (Benjet, Azar, & Kuersten-Hogan, 2003). Traditional psychological tests can, however, be useful in measuring characteristics that may explain a parent's caregiving deficits, even though they do not measure parenting capacity itself. For example, an MMPI may be informative in identifying serious depression in a parent who manifests poor ability to manage stress in parenting situations. (See Table 5.4 for a selective list of traditional psychological tests.)

BEHAVIORAL AND MENTAL HEALTH SYMPTOMS TESTS

Tests such as the BDI-II, SCL-90-R, and BSI may be useful when MHPs seek to supplement interview data regarding the presence or absence of specific mental health symptoms. Each of these tests has been standardized, has clinical norms for different populations, and measures constructs often relevant to parenting capacity evaluations.

Table 5.4 | Traditional Psychological Tests for Potential Use in Parenting Capacity Evaluations

Measures of Behavioral and Mental Health Symptoms
- Beck Depression Inventory–second edition (BDI-II) (Beck, Steer & Brown, 1996)
- Symptom Checklist-90–Revised (SCL-90-R) (Derogatis, 1994)
- Brief Symptom Inventory (BSI) (Derogatis, 1993)

Measures of Intelligence and Achievement Levels
- Wechsler Adult Intelligence Scale–fourth edition (WAIS-IV) (Wechsler, 2008)
- Wechsler Abbreviated Scale of Intelligence (WASI) (Wechsler, 1999)
- Stanford-Binet Intelligence Scale–fourth edition (Thorndike, Hagen, & Sattler, 1986)
- Wide Range Achievement Test–fourth edition (WRAT-IV) (Wilkinson & Robertson, 2006)
- Wechsler Individual Achievement Test (WIAT-II) (Wechsler, 1992)

Measures of Personality Functioning
- Minnesota Multiphasic Personality Inventory–2 (MMPI-2) (Butcher, Graham, Ben-Porath, Tellegen, Dahlstrom & Kaemmer, 2001) and MMPI-2-RF (Restructured Form) (Ben-Porath & Tellegen, 2008)
- Personality Assessment Inventory (PAI) (Morey, 1991)
- Millon Clinical Multiaxial Inventory–III (MCMI-III) (Millon, 1997)

5 chapter

However, MHPs should keep in mind that elevated scores may reflect symptoms related to the examinee's involvement with child protection services and court or other aspects of living, rather than parenting deficits per se. These checklists contribute to an objective assessment of the degree of symptoms acknowledged by the examinee but do not necessarily imply impairment in specific functional capacities. Furthermore, results suggesting an absence of symptoms should be interpreted cautiously as well, in that they are all self-report measures and do not account for response style or self-presentation bias.

INTELLIGENCE AND ACHIEVEMENT TESTS

Cognitive and psycho-educational tests may be useful when MHPs have concern about a parent's intellectual or academic functioning, and reliable information on the nature of the deficits is not available through another source. Often, cognitive testing already has been done on parents referred for FMHA, and, if the testing was conducted fairly recently, there is usually no reason to suspect that the results of previous assessment would change. However, there are occasionally situations, such as the assessment of teenage parents, in which formal testing has never been done and is directly useful. For example, a parent with limited expressive-language facility might be suspected either of having overall cognitive deficits or a receptive language delay, and the results would have different implications for the forensic evaluation. When assessing adolescent parents, MHPs should consider that testing, even if conducted in the last year, might not be sufficient, because an adolescent's functioning can change considerably over the course of a year.

There are instances in which it is necessary to determine the presence or absence of mental retardation or a learning disability. For example, in termination-of-parental-rights cases, when one of the referral questions is whether a parent has a diagnosable mental impairment, such information is relevant. In addition to a test of intelligence, assessment of adaptive functioning, through a measure such as the Vineland Adaptive Behavior Scales, second edition (Sparrow, Balla, & Cicchetti, 2005), is necessary if the referral question focuses on whether the parent meets criteria for a diagnosis of mental retardation. Diagnostic determinations, such as mental retardation, can be helpful in explaining the conditions responsible for limitations or strengths in parenting functioning. However, diagnostic determinations are not a substitute for direct information on parenting strengths and weaknesses.

PERSONALITY TESTS

Tests of personality functioning may be useful in parenting capacity evaluations to augment other data sources (i.e., interviews, records, collateral contacts) regarding the parent's personality and behavior. For example, when MHPs are faced with a parent displaying paranoid tendencies that hinder the ability to conduct a thorough interview, personality tests may assist in differentiating between situational guardedness or mistrust and true clinical paranoia. Personality tests may also assist MHPs in assessing factors that may be impairing parenting, such as underlying hostility or anger, self-absorption or grandiosity, or antisocial tendencies. As noted by Budd and Holdsworth (1996), MHPs should not use personality tests with the intent of assessing parenting ability itself. Given that court-involved individuals often produce invalid profiles (i.e., elevated validity indexes) on personality tests, clinicians should consider the possible impact of validity scale scores on interpretation of the clinical scales (see discussion in Chapter 3).

Tests of Parenting

Tests of parenting are potentially useful in assessment of parenting capacity due to the fact that their item content is directly relevant to the areas being assessed. Parenting tests are designed variously to assess childrearing knowledge, attitudes, beliefs, abilities, behaviors, and styles. Despite their relevance of content, virtually all parenting tests were designed for purposes other than forensic assessment in child-protection cases, which limits their interpretability for the FMHA. In addition, few have validity scales, thus eliminating the ability to assess response style, and few have been assessed with regard to their ability to meet scientific and evidentiary standards. Table 5.5 lists some of the available tests of parenting and their characteristics. Most of these tests were included in a

Table 5.5 | Tests of Parenting

Title	Constructs Assessed	Reading Level	Validity Scales	Relevance to Forensic Issues	References
Adult-Adolescent Parenting Inventory (AAPI-2)*	Parents' and pre-parents' behaviors and attitudes known to be attributable to abuse and neglect	5th grade	No		Bavolek & Keene (1999)
Alabama Parenting Questionnaire (APQ)	Parenting practices related to disruptive behavior problems		No		Shelton, Frick, & Wootton (1996)
Child Abuse Potential Inventory (CAPI)*	Risk for physical child abuse	3rd grade	Yes	Yes (Otto & Edens, 2003; Yanez & Fremouw, 2004)	Milner (1986, 1990, 1994)
Parent Awareness Skills Survey (PASS)*	Parents' under-standing of how to handle typical parenting respon-sibilities		No	No (Erickson, Lillienfeld, & Vitacco, 2007; Otto & Edens, 2003)	Bricklin (1990)
Parent Behavior Checklist (PBC)	Family strengths and needs; how parents are raising their children ages one to five years; parenting strengths and weaknesses	3rd grade	No		Fox (1994)
Parent–Child Relationship Inventory (PCRI)*	Parents' attitudes regarding parent-ing and children; for children between 3 and 15 years	4th grade	Yes	No (Otto & Edens, 2003; Yanez & Fremouw, 2004)	Gerard (1994)

Parent Perception of Child Profile (PPCP)*	Parents' awareness and understanding child development across various stages		No	No (Erickson et al., 2007; Otto & Edens, 2003)	Bricklin & Elliott (1991)
Parent Opinion Questionnaire (POQ)*	Age-appropriateness of parents' expectations of a child's behaviors		No		Azar, Robinson, Hekimian, & Twentyman (1984); Azar & Rohrbeck (1986); Budd, Heilman, & Kane (2000)
Parenting Satisfaction Scale (PSS)	Parents' level of satisfaction in and attitudes toward parenting		No		Guidubaldi & Cleminshaw (1988)
Parenting Scale (PS)	Dysfunctional discipline practices in parents of children up to age four		No		Arnold, O'Leary, Wolff, & Acker (1993)
Parenting Stress Index– third edition (PSI and PSI-SF)*	Parent–child systems that are under stress and at risk for dysfunctional parenting behavior or behavior problems in the child ages one month to 12 years	5th grade	Yes	Yes (Otto & Edens, 2003; Yanez & Fremouw, 2004)	Abidin (1995); Abidin, Flens, & Austin (2006)
Stress Index for Parents of Adolescents (SIPA)	Stressful areas in parent–adolescent interactions in parents of adolescents ages 11 to 19 years	5th grade	No		Sheras, Abidin, & Konold (1998)

* Denotes measures discussed in research review in Chapter 3.

detailed review of the conceptual bases, development, and psychometric properties of parenting measures relative to forensic assessment (Otto & Edens, 2003). Parenting tests frequently used by forensic practitioners in child protection evaluations are discussed in Chapter 3, along with evidence regarding their validity. The column labeled "Relevance to Forensic Issues" cites review articles discussing the scientific support (or lack thereof) for various tests.

An MHP's choice to administer any of the measures listed in Table 5.5 should factor in the reading level, content relevance, and age specifications. As noted in the table, only the CAPI and the PSI have been reviewed as having sufficient standardization, validity, and peer-reviewed research to support their use in forensic assessment at the present time. As such, these tests are recommended for use in parenting capacity evaluations. Further information about each of these measures is provided in the sections that follow.

CAPI

The Child Abuse Potential Inventory is a 160-item self-report measure designed as a screening device to identify characteristics that are often found in or shared with known physical abusers. The measure contains items related to parents' beliefs about parenting, their expectations of their children, and their personal functioning. The CAPI contains validity scales that provide measures of faking-good, faking-bad, and random responding. Responses yield an overall score on the Abuse Scale, which is subdivided into six factor scales: Distress, Rigidity, Unhappiness, Parent–Child Problems, Problems with Family Members, and Problems with Others. Of note is that elevated abuse scale scores can still be interpreted if a profile is invalid due to "faking-good." The CAPI was constructed and validated with a population of known physically abusive parents. Use of the test with the general population, or with a population whose base rate of physical abuse is lower than 50 percent, is not advised, as there is risk for high false-positive rates (Milner, 1986). Of course, MHPs should never draw conclusions about abuse potential on the basis of CAPI scores alone.

PSI

The Parenting Stress Index, third edition, is a 120-item self-report measure that assists in identifying parent–child systems under stress and at risk for dysfunctional parenting behavior or behavior problems in the child. There is also a short form (PSI-SF) that contains 36 items. Both are designed to be used with parents of children aged one month to 12 years, with the parent completing the items as they pertain to a specific child. The PSI and PSI-SF provide information about defensive responding, total stress in the parenting role, child factors contributing to stress, parent factors contributing to stress, and overall stress related to circumstances beyond the parent's control. The PSI and PSI-SF have been validated with a variety of American samples, as well as with international groups (Abidin, 1995). Abidin et al. (2006) raised concern about limitations related to the normative sample that included only mothers from a limited cultural background and a non-forensic population. However, Reitman, Currier, and Stickle's (2002) examination of the psychometric qualities of the PSI-SF with low-income and predominantly African American mothers supported the use of the test with this population.

Also necessary for MHPs to consider when administering the PSI is the interpretation of scores when the parent is not living with or actively parenting the child. In these situations, elevated scores may reflect stress related to separation rather than caregiving. Alternatively, parents may obtain normative scores that suggest the absence of problems, but these scores may relate to the fact that the parent is not responsible for full-time caregiving. Milner and Crouch (1997) also noted that, in their research, "misclassification rates in the fake-good condition exceeded 50 percent, which suggest that the PSI Defensive Responding Scale has limited utility in detecting individual cases of faking-good behavior" (p. 645).

Some tests of parenting included in Table 5.5 have been reviewed and assessed as *not* meeting scientific standards (i.e., the PASS, PCRI, and PPCP), and thus are not recommended for use in parenting capacity evaluations. Most other tests of parenting

5
chapter

have not been studied with regard to their reliability and validity in a forensic context. Some (e.g., AAPI and POQ) have been subjected to empirical evaluation with at-risk or maltreating parents, but evidence is mixed regarding their factor structure and/or validity. As discussed in Chapter 3, measures that fall in this category should be used with extreme caution if at all.

Testing Methodology

Testing can be administered at any point in the assessment process. Conducting testing early in the process can assist MHPs in developing hypotheses that can then guide future data gathering. It can also be a less threatening beginning to the evaluation for a parent than face-to-face interviewing and having to answer challenging questions directly from the evaluator. On the other hand, merely using testing because it is a convenient start to the assessment can lead to more testing than is necessary. If MHPs wait to conduct testing until they have gathered the majority of data from other sources, they may learn that testing would not provide necessary information beyond what has otherwise been obtained.

For self-report measures, administration should be closely monitored by the evaluator or a technician for attention, alertness, and concentration of the examinee while completing the measure, and to ensure that no external factors influenced administration. MHPs should strictly adhere to standardized administration and scoring procedures and, if variation occurs for any reason, consider the effects in reporting their results (Heilbrun, 2001; Standards for Educational and Psychological Testing, 1999).

Factoring In Positive-Impression Management

As discussed in the review of research on forensic measures in Chapter 3, it is not uncommon for parents undergoing testing as part of a parenting capacity evaluation to produce invalid profiles due to "faking good." Efforts at impression management may be a normal response to court-ordered parent evaluations. MHPs should consider using measures of impression management or corroborative information when it comes time to decide whether and how much to rely on the examinee's self-report information. There is no basis for assuming that the individual would have produced this profile in a non-compelled evaluation setting. Carr, Moretti, and Cue (2005) noted that "the validity-scale elevations can reasonably be understood as resulting from the demands of the test situation, and conclusions about client traits based on these elevations may be ill founded" (p. 194). Because it is difficult to interpret elevations on validity indices, they often render the profile invalid. When this occurs, the evaluator must acknowledge that it is not possible to interpret the test results and explain why.

Projective personality tests were reviewed in Chapter 3 as generally lacking in empirical support for forensic assessment purposes. Nevertheless, some in the field have argued that one potential advantage of using the Rorschach Inkblot Method in parenting capacity evaluations is the instrument's resistance to impression management (Weiner, 2006). The Rorschach Inkblot Method may provide information about characteristics pertinent to parenting capacity, such as general level of adjustment, adequacy of coping skills, and interpersonal accessibility, and responses may be less prone to the influence of impression management. Given the controversy regarding the measure, however, MHPs should be well versed in the literature so as to be able to support their decision to administer the test.

Summary

This chapter has provided information about the data collection steps for conducting parenting capacity evaluations and critical factors to consider for each step. Fundamental to a forensically sound evaluation is the use of multiple methods and data sources that typically include records, interviews with examinees, interviews with third-party or collateral sources, and observations of parents with their children. Tests and child interviews sometimes add relevant additional information. Although the outlined components are useful for completing a thorough evaluation, the referral questions should ultimately guide data gathering. When a

5
chapter

desired source of data is not available, MHPs should be sure to document their attempts to gather the information and note any limitations of their conclusions as a result. Finally, throughout the data-gathering process, it is vital for MHPs to assess the relevance of each data source as well as the reliability of the data gathered.

Interpretation | 6

O nce data for a forensic mental health assessment have been collected, evaluators are faced with the challenge of integrating and assigning meaning to the information. Interpreting findings about parenting capability is complicated by the lack of criteria for determining minimal parental fitness (Budd, 2001), the potential for evaluator bias to influence evaluations (Azar, Lauretti, & Loding, 1998), and the uncertainty inherent in drawing conclusions about the future when relying on past events. One forensic writer noted the complexity of the task of establishing a "coherent way of describing and characterizing the many areas of emotional, cognitive, social, and behavioral functioning" involved in parenting (Barnum, 1997, p. 587).

This chapter outlines and discusses the steps for integrating and interpreting data, taking into account the challenges inherent in conducting parenting capacity evaluations. The steps are to (1) consider the referral questions; (2) develop working hypotheses; (3) consider supporting and contradictory data for working hypotheses; (4) consider the reliability and validity of data; (5) attend to inconsistencies, gaps, and limitations in data; (6) consider the broader context of the family; and (7) draw conclusions and make recommendations. In confronting this final step, evaluators must determine whether or how to address the *ultimate legal issue*—the question before the court. Approaches are suggested for forensic evaluators to provide clear and useful conclusions that touch on issues of risk and protection rather than to offer an opinion on the ultimate decision to be made by the court.

Consider the Referral Questions

Given the volume of information typically collected in child protection cases, sifting through it to identify meaningful facts and observations can seem like a daunting task. In order to effectively and efficiently go about this task, a necessary first step is to review the data in light of the referral questions and determine which data are *relevant* to those questions. Not all data collected will serve to inform conclusions, nor will all the data be presented in the report. The focus on relevance is consistent with the principle put forth by the "Specialty Guidelines for Forensic Psychologists" (hereinafter referred to as Specialty Guidelines) (Committee on Professional Guidelines for Forensic Psychologists, 1991) that mental health professionals "avoid offering information from their investigations or evaluations that does not bear directly upon the legal purpose of their professional services and that is not critical as support for their product, evidence, [or] testimony" (p. 662). For example, in conducting an evaluation to assist the court in determining the appropriateness of unsupervised day visits between a mother and child, data regarding the mother's emotional state and parenting skills during supervised visits would be extremely relevant information, whereas data regarding the mother's employment history may not. If the purpose of the evaluation were to assist the court in determining if the child should be returned home, the mother's employment history would then be pertinent, as it would pertain to her capacity to provide stability for her child.

Grisso's model of legal competencies (2003), as described in Chapter 2, provides a useful framework within which evaluators can begin to identify relevant data. MHPs should attend to information that offers insight into the parent's *functioning* in the parenting role (e.g., what the parent understands, believes, knows, does, and is capable of doing related to parenting). Also important is information that pertains to the probable reasons or *causes* for the deficits in functional abilities, such as life-situational stress, examination stress, ambivalence about parenting, lack of information, or a mental disorder or disability (Otto & Edens, 2003). Keeping in mind that the significance of a parenting weakness or deficit will depend on the specific needs of the child (Otto & Edens, 2003), evaluators should also highlight findings that pertain to the *interaction* between the parent's functional abilities and the task demands of the situation.

BEST PRACTICE
When interpreting data, be sure to consider the referral questions and whether the data collected are relevant to the issues at hand. The data should offer insight into the parent's functioning and probable causes for any parenting deficits.

Develop Working Hypotheses

Once MHPs have framed the evaluation within the scope of the referral issues, the next step is to develop working hypotheses about the case. These hypotheses should be clearly linked to the referral questions. For example, if the referral source is seeking information about a depressed mother's capacity to care for her child who has cerebral palsy, as the evaluator gathers information, a potential working hypothesis might be, "The mother's depression causes her to be unable to take care of her own needs and thus unable to take care of her child's special needs." If the referral source is seeking information about the likelihood that a father with a lengthy substance-abuse history could make the gains necessary to achieve the return home of his four children, a potential working hypothesis might be, "The father's current low risk of relapse associated with treatment compliance decreases the risk that he would further neglect his children." Testing results can also be useful "for generating hypotheses worthy of further investigation or consideration" (Melton et al., 2007, p. 51). For example, if a parent's responses on the Child Abuse Potential Inventory yielded an elevated score on the Abuse Index, the evaluator could then hypothesize that the parent is at increased risk for engaging in physically abusive behavior.

While working hypotheses are being developed, MHPs utilize data collected from multiple sources to make interpretations, and when supported, clinical inferences. Tippins and Wittmann (2005) offered a four-level model for making clinical inferences, in which evaluators proceed from descriptive statements to conclusions, in child custody evaluations. This model is also relevant to child protection evaluations and is described briefly here. At *Level I*, evaluators focus on making observations and interpreting what they have observed through the lens of empirical and clinical knowledge. In the case of a parenting capacity evaluation, this could include observations such as, "The mother expressed reluctance to participate in the evaluation," or "The caseworker reported that the father is committed to engaging in ongoing visitation." A large proportion of the typical FMHA report consists of Level I observations.

At *Level II*, evaluators begin to make interpretations based on these observations and, weaving together strands of consistent and inconsistent data, make "inferences about the presence, absence, or severity of general psychological constructs" (Tippins & Wittmann, 2005, p. 196). In the case of a parenting capacity evaluation, this could include inferences such as, "The mother harbors mistrust toward those in positions of authority," or "The father is emotionally attached to his son."

At *Level III*, evaluators begin to draw conclusions about the implications of these inferences, thus providing the court with information that may influence decision making. In the case of a parenting capacity evaluation, this could include conclusions such as, "The mother's mistrust places her at risk for noncompliance with parenting services, and thus, at risk for not making necessary parenting gains," or "The father's positive attachment suggests a capacity to display adequate empathy toward his son."

Finally, at *Level IV*, evaluators make statements about what should happen. In the case of a parenting

INFO

Four levels of inference by Tippins and Wittmann:

- Level I—what the clinician observes
- Level II—what the clinician concludes about the psychology of a parent, child, or family
- Level III—what the clinician concludes about the implications of these inferences
- Level IV—what the clinician recommends

capacity evaluation, this could include statements such as, "The mother should not be reunited with her daughter," or "The father should regain custody of his son." Of note, Tippins and Wittmann recommend limited use of Level III inferences, and they do not recommend that evaluators draw conclusions at Level IV (this principle is discussed in greater detail later in this chapter).

Given the import of accuracy of information in forensic evaluations, interpretative statements need to be carefully considered. According to Tippins and Wittman (2005), MHPs should be cautious about moving from Level I and II observations and interpretations to Level III inferences. At Levels I and II, MHPs are able to apply clinical and empirical knowledge and engage in "a rigorous hypothesis-testing approach" so that "cautious psychological conclusions can be drawn to assist the finder of fact in sorting through contradictory allegations" (Tippins & Wittmann, 2005, p. 197). Tippins and Wittmann noted that Level III conclusions should be clearly grounded in case-specific facts, and that, beyond statements of risk and advantage, "there is little that can be reliably said by mental health professionals" (p. 201) about the implications of inferences for decisions about parenting capacity. Evaluators are more helpful to the court when they couch findings in behavioral rather than traditional diagnostic or clinical terms (such as "bipolar disorder" or "defensive") that may connote unexpected and even incorrect information to the court. Any clinical observations or findings are relevant only in terms of the specific ways they affect parenting capacity, and it is this nexus that must be clear to the evaluator and to the court.

Consider Supporting and Contradictory Data for Working Hypotheses

As evaluators review collected data, it is critical to do so objectively and to attend to data that both support and refute working hypotheses. MHPs should not adopt a stance (e.g., for or against a parent's caregiving ability) and attempt to verify or support it with the data, but rather they should strive to let the data inform their opinions. According to the Specialty Guidelines (1991),

"The forensic psychologist maintains professional integrity by examining the issue at hand from all reasonable perspectives, actively seeking information that will differentially test plausible rival hypotheses" (p. 661). Evaluators must actively work to avoid premature conclusions, being mindful of the potential for biases to distort judgments about the meaning of data. Tippins and Wittmann (2005) cited literature that highlights clinicians' susceptibility to distortions in observation as well as the potential for inaccuracy in recording data in forensic evaluations. To the extent that evaluators are aware of their own inherent biases (e.g., regarding physical appearance, language facility, ethnicity, socioeconomic status, or other variables), they can make efforts to reduce the potential for these automatic reactions to affect their interpretation of data.

As noted throughout this volume, the evaluation of parenting capacity in child protection matters is complicated by the lack of consensus in both social science and legal realms regarding the abilities required for adequate parenting. Evaluators are ethically obligated to respect individual and cultural differences in assessing parenting practices (American Psychological Association, 2002; American Psychological Association Committee on Professional Practice and Standards, 1999). However, in the absence of universally accepted minimal parenting standards, MHPs "are susceptible to employing vague and subjective criteria based on their personal experience" (Budd, 2001, p. 3) when drawing conclusions about parenting practices. Compounding this susceptibility is the dearth of appropriate testing instruments in the field to assess parenting-related constructs (see Chapters 3 and 5 for further discussion) (Budd, 2001). Without valid and reliable measures of parenting constructs, evaluators are often left to apply their own definitions of "minimal parenting" standards.

BEWARE
Be objective when reviewing data. Do not let your personal views or biases inform your opinion.

MHPs can take steps in the data-reviewing process to decrease the likelihood of any bias impacting their interpretation. Pezzot-Pearce and Pearce (2004) suggested making summary sheets that outline the reason for the referral and the working hypotheses. Systematically reviewing the data and noting on these sheets evidence that supports and refutes the hypotheses may decrease the potential for biases by assuring that the evaluator incorporates *all* information.

Utilizing an organizational method like this will also assist evaluators in supporting conclusions with citations of specific data points.

Consider the Reliability and Validity of Data

MHPs should consider the strength and convergence of collected data across sources and measures in order to draw sound and credible conclusions. As discussed in Chapter 5, Heilbrun (2001) recommended selectivity in choosing data sources, noting that information with low reliability (i.e., believability) will not increase the overall accuracy of the evaluation and may, if given much weight, decrease the reliability of one's conclusions. Factors to consider when assessing the reliability and validity at each stage of the data-collection process (i.e., record review, interviews, collateral contacts, parent–child observation, and testing) are highlighted in Table 6.1.

One of the most common challenges facing evaluators in assessing the reliability of data is the tendency of parents to attempt to portray themselves in a favorable light. This tendency, although natural in compelled examinations, may be exaggerated to the extent that it affects the reliability of the data collected in interviews, observations, and testing. Attempts at positive-impression management may include extreme guardedness and reluctance to participate or answer questions, minimization or denial of faults or responsibility for past mistakes, presentation of misinformation,

6 chapter

Table 6.1 | Factors That May Limit Validity and Reliability of Data

Records:
- Data from secondary sources
- Incomplete or illegible records
- Potential for inaccurate or biased information
- Source going beyond scope of expertise

Interviews with parents:
- Only able to conduct one interview
- Positive-impression management by parent
- Mental status concerns
- Anxiety about being evaluated
- Language and/or cultural barriers

Collateral interviews:
- Reluctance to participate
- Lack of objectivity
- Lack of specific expertise
- Suggestibility
- Memory loss
- Opinions based on limited or incomplete data

Parent–child observations:
- Positive-impression management by parent
- Coaching of child
- Methodological concerns (short in duration; conducted in unnatural setting)

Testing:
- Positive-impression management by parent
- Lack of objective measures of test-taker attitude
- Necessity for inferential leap from test results to parenting issues
- Lack of generalizability from normative group to examinees

or extreme talkativeness and agreeableness. The task of evaluators when faced with such presentations is to assess the reasons for them and gauge the extent to which they color or obfuscate the findings. MHPs should ask themselves questions like the following: (1) How much is this presentation a function of true lack of insight? (2) How much is it related to personality characteristics or mental status concerns? (3) How much is it related to fear or mistrust of the child protection system? (4) How much is it a culturally syntonic way of interacting with professionals from the larger culture?

Attend to Inconsistencies, Gaps, and Limitations in Data

It is not uncommon for evaluators to identify inconsistencies in the data collected; all of the information will rarely fit together neatly. Some inconsistencies can be cleared up by further inquiry, but others will remain unresolved. For example, in a case involving alleged domestic violence between parents, the MHP may find information that both supports and refutes the allegation. As a result, the MHP is unable to make a clear statement about risk of future violence in the family, and thus about the risk of future inadequate care for the child. When faced with this type of inconsistent data, the role of the evaluator is to attempt to understand which information is plausible rather than to conclusively resolve the inconsistencies (Melton et al., 2007). In this way, the MHP can provide the court with some guidance in filtering information relevant to considerations regarding the alleged atmosphere of family violence. The evaluator should present the contradictory data and explain why a firm conclusion cannot be drawn. The evaluator should also outline conclusions if more information is obtained; for example, stating the level of risk if in fact the domestic violence did occur and the level of risk if it did not.

It is also not uncommon to encounter gaps in the data collected. For example, in cases involving physical harm to a child (e.g., broken bones), it may have been determined at adjudication that abuse occurred, but not who perpetrated the abuse. When evaluators are asked to assess parenting capacity in such cases, they will not have full information about what actually occurred and who harmed the child. The absence of such important details can make the task of determining risk and protective issues extremely difficult and sometimes impossible. In such cases, it is critical that the MHP draw conclusions cautiously and articulate clearly the rationale for exercising caution for each conclusion reached.

It is critical that evaluators note any limitations in the data that have been collected, and thus, any limitations in the conclusions they draw. The importance of articulating limitations is highlighted by both the Specialty Guidelines (1991) and the psychologists'

BEST PRACTICE

Substantiate opinions or conclusions with information from multiple sources, giving more weight to data from more reliable sources.

Ethics Code (American Psychological Association, 2002). According to the Specialty Guidelines, "Forensic psychologists... have an affirmative responsibility to acknowledge the uncorroborated status of... data and the reasons for relying upon such data" (p. 662). Furthermore, when unable to conduct an examination of an individual adequate to the scope of conclusions to be drawn, forensic psychologists "make clear the impact of such limitations on the reliability and validity of their professional products, evidence, or testimony" (p. 663). The Ethics Code notes that psychologists should take into account factors "that might... reduce the accuracy of their interpretations [and] indicate any significant limitations of their interpretations" (p. 24).

Given many of the potential limitations inherent in parenting capacity evaluations, as well as the high stakes of such evaluations, it is recommended that evaluators err on the side of conservatively interpreting findings. Evaluators should only make interpretations that are supported by the data, should always seek convergent data across sources, and should firmly ground their conclusions in specific data points (Budd & Holdsworth, 1996; Heilbrun, 2001; Melton et al., 2007).

Consider the Broader Context of the Family

MHPs must consider factors at the level of the child, parent, and environment within which the family lives when assessing conditions impacting parenting. Approaching the interpretation of findings from a systems framework is consistent with Bronfenbrenner's (1979) ecological systems theory, as described in Chapter 3. The case vignettes provided in the sections that follow illustrate the importance of grounding interpretation in the specific context of each family.

Case Vignette #1

A Spanish-speaking mother has lost custody of her two children due to neglect. The children are placed in a bilingual foster home, and as a result, they are losing their ability to speak Spanish. The caseworker describes the mother as "resistant" to her English language classes. Currently the mother lives with extended family members, and the caseworker expresses concern about the mother's "refusal" to provide information about the people living in her home and notes the mother is becoming less "open." The caseworker recommends permanency with the foster parents.

In this case, the evaluator learns that the mother is unable to attend language classes because they take place at night when she is reluctant to leave her home due to gang violence in the neighborhood. The mother expresses distrust of her caseworker and notes she is reluctant to provide information about her family members due to their illegal immigration status. By considering the broader cultural and environmental context of the mother's actions, the evaluator is able to gain a clearer understanding of the reasons for the mother's behavior (i.e., realistic fear for her safety and concern for the well-being of her family). In parenting capacity evaluations, it is critical that evaluators, when interpreting noncompliance by parents, first consider the strategies that have been used to engage parents, rather than immediately conclude that noncompliance is representative of a lack of concern for a child (Azar & Benjet, 1994).

Case Vignette #2

A three-year-old child cries during supervised visits with her father. The foster parents report that after the visits the child engages in defiant behavior and experiences nightmares. The therapist has reported concerns to the court about the child's continuing to visit with the father, and the caseworker is also concerned that these visits may be too disruptive and may be straining the foster home placement.

During the evaluation of the case described here, the evaluator learns that the foster mother discusses her dislike of the father in front of the child as well as her belief that the child is afraid of him. The foster mother participates in the child's therapy sessions and shares these concerns with the therapist as well. In addition, the foster mother accompanies the child to the supervised visits. When the evaluator discusses the concerns with the father, he indicates that he does not know what to do when his child cries during visits and often just disengages because the foster mother steps in. In this case, conclusions about the father's parenting capacity will need to include consideration of the child's developmental age and age expected reactions to separation issues and the influence of the foster mother on the child at home and during visits. If the evaluator simply considered the child's behaviors and the father's actions, potentially erroneous conclusions could be drawn (i.e., that the child is afraid of the father and that the father is not interested in improving his interactions with his child).

Draw Conclusions and Make Recommendations

The evaluator has now identified the relevant data, identified information that supports or refutes working hypotheses, and clearly attended to any limitations present in the data. The final step is to draw conclusions and make recommendations that will be useful to the referral source without going beyond the scope of the evaluation. Conclusions should be grounded in the theoretical constructs discussed in detail in Chapter 3 and should incorporate the evaluator's clinical knowledge and judgment about parenting strengths and weaknesses, children's development and needs, and risk and protective factors (as outlined in Chapter 4).

BEST PRACTICE

Avoid offering conclusions that are not clearly grounded in case-specific facts. Base any conclusions made on your specialized knowledge base, the needs of the child, and the related risk and protective factors.

Opinions on the Ultimate Issue

There are differing views in the field about whether forensic evaluators should offer an opinion on the ultimate legal issue (i.e., the legal question to be answered by the judge or jury). Some authors have opined that forensic evaluators should *not* do so (Grisso, 2003; Heilbrun, 2001; Melton et al., 2007; Otto & Edens, 2003), arguing that "the ultimate legal question, which includes moral, political, and community values, should not be the focus of the evaluation's conclusion" (Heilbrun et al., 2007, p. 55). However, as summarized by Budd and Springman (in press), other authors have questioned the practicality of refraining from offering ultimate-issue opinions for several reasons. Notably, they observe that judicial officials prefer to hear specific recommendations from mental health professionals. Furthermore, judges bear the responsibility to weigh ultimate-issue opinions against all available evidence. The authors also observe that mental health professionals have relevant expertise on family dynamics, and their opinions may be of assistance to the court. Additionally, when mental health professionals make explicit recommendations, these may facilitate out-of-court settlements; for example, in child custody disputes. Heilbrun (2001) noted that avoiding conclusions about the ultimate legal issue could lead to exclusion of the entire evaluation or reduction in the weight of the evidence.

Some, but not all, referrals for evaluations of parenting capacity specifically include a request that the evaluator weigh in on the ultimate legal issue. As discussed in Chapter 4, evaluators should clarify in advance with the referral source what questions can and cannot be realistically addressed in a parenting capacity evaluation. Budd and Springman (in press) provided an analysis of the directness of evaluators' recommendations in parenting capacity evaluations as they related to the referral questions. They found that direct recommendations were more likely to be offered in response to narrow, statute-based issues (e.g., termination of parental rights, capacity to consent to adoption) and less likely to be offered for other referral issues (e.g., evaluation of parental functioning for service planning, permanency goals, visitation arrangements, progress in services). Budd and Springman noted that adding to the complexity of weighing in on the ultimate legal issue are the lack of a clear definition of what constitutes "good enough" parenting, lack of clear guidelines about how to weigh parenting risks against strengths, and limited direction about how to apply the theoretical construct of a child's best interests to the circumstances of individual cases.

Articulating Risks and Protective Factors

Tippins and Wittmann (2005), in their discussion of a model for making clinical inferences in child-custody evaluations, recommended that clinicians "include a summary for the court of notable psychological risks and/or advantages associated with various access plans" (p. 200) rather than making statements about the ultimate legal issue. For example, an evaluator assessing a parent's capacity related to a decision about termination of parental rights could discuss the functional characteristics of the parent that indicate whether he or she is able or unable to carry out basic parenting tasks and meet his or her child's needs. However, specifically stating the opinion that the parent's rights should or should not be terminated might be inappropriate. Furthermore, the evaluator should clearly discuss the evidence about potential causes for deficits in functional parenting characteristics, both to provide supporting data and to assist in determining whether the parent's deficits are remediable (Otto & Edens, 2003). Evaluators can also discuss issues of parenting capacity in terms of "likelihood" rather than more definitive statements, to reflect the inherent uncertainty of the conclusions. For example, in the above example, the evaluator could express the opinion that "it is likely [or unlikely] that the parent will be able to successfully parent the child" and provide descriptive evidence to support the statement. In some cases, due to limitations in the data beyond the control of the evaluator, a clear conclusion regarding the level of risk or "likelihood" of one outcome or another cannot be made.

In such cases, evaluators should clearly articulate that the data do not support one opinion more than another, and specify what data, if gathered, would provide greater clarity.

How the evaluator presents conclusions will be guided by the way the referral questions are posed. As discussed in Chapter 4, understanding the purpose for which the evaluation was sought (i.e., what will the evaluation help to determine) will help the evaluator frame the answers and conclusions. For example, if an evaluation is requested to assist in determining the appropriateness of moving from supervised to unsupervised visitation, the evaluator would want to address risk and protective factors related to the parent's having limited unsupervised time with the child, probably during the day. If, however, the evaluation is to assist with determining if a child should be immediately returned home, the evaluator would need to address risk and protective factors related to the parent's meeting the child's needs on a full-time basis.

Risk factors should not be considered in isolation but should be viewed in company with the potentially mitigating impact of protective factors. For example, an evaluator might note that the risk associated with a mother's longstanding and severe history of physical abuse of her children is mitigated by her current sobriety and the assessment that all incidents of abuse occurred when she was actively abusing substances. Likewise, protective factors should be viewed in company with the potentially adverse impact of risk factors. For example, an evaluator might note that, despite the mother and father's engaging in ongoing therapy to address their history of domestic violence and harming their children, their tendency to blame external factors or each other for their actions suggests that the risk of ongoing harm is significant.

The number of risk or protective factors is not as important as the nature of the factors. For example, protective factors suggesting that a mother is able to adequately parent her daughter may include her engagement in therapy to address her husband's sexual abuse of her daughter, her insight into the impact of her own sexual-abuse history on her failure to protect her daughter, her consistent visits with her daughter and cooperation with caseworkers, results of a self-report measure indicating limited stress related to parenting, the apparently strong emotional connection between her and her daughter, and her extensive support network of family and friends. However, her plan to keep her husband actively involved in parenting, including allowing him unsupervised access to their daughter, significantly weakens the level of protection conferred by the other factors.

Frequently, evaluators are asked to provide service recommendations as part of parenting capacity evaluations. Recommendations should reflect the specific risks and parenting concerns outlined in the body of the evaluation. For example, if an identified risk is a mother's current untreated manic symptoms, a recommendation for psychiatric intervention would be appropriate. Or, if a father displays that he has difficulty in setting effective limits for his defiant child, an intervention such as parent coaching to help him improve his skills would be appropriate. It is also important that evaluators incorporate protective factors and parenting strengths into recommendations when possible. For example, if a young mother receives significant emotional and parenting support from her aunt, the evaluator may recommend that the aunt participate in family therapy sessions.

When making recommendations, evaluators should also factor in the parent's past cooperation with treatment, whether it is realistic for the parent to complete the services (e.g., due to scheduling constraints, location of services, and the parent's ability to travel), if the parent has ever been given access to adequate resources and services, whether the parent has benefited from services in the past, and the parent's willingness to comply. An unwillingness or apparent inability to comply with traditional intervention may (or may not) justify not recommending the intervention, but the reasons should be clearly stated for curtailing recommendations that would otherwise be made. Additionally, alternative recommendations for accomplishing the necessary remediation should, whenever possible, be offered.

Summary

Integrating and interpreting data for parenting capacity evaluations can be a daunting task, replete with challenges inherent to child protection matters. MHPs can take steps to address these challenges and present the referral source with relevant, reliable, and useful information. Such steps include maintaining their focus on the reason for referral and sifting through the data to identify pertinent information; attending to all of the data collected, not just data that support any one hypothesis; clearly supporting all conclusions with data; identifying limitations in the data or methodology of the evaluation; and interpreting data within the broader context of the family. Finally, MHPs should err on the side of conservatively interpreting findings. That is, MHPs should avoid offering conclusions that are not clearly grounded in case-specific facts. Finally, any inferences made should be based on the evaluator's specialized knowledge base.

Report Writing and Testimony | 7

The final task in forensic mental health assessment involves communicating the results, which entails translating clinical knowledge into a legally useful form. Virtually all court-ordered evaluations and most referred from attorneys or caseworkers result in the preparation of written reports, whereas only a subset requires oral testimony. Expert testimony is generally less common in child protection cases than in many other legal contexts. Although practices vary by jurisdiction, the typical conditions of child protection work (e.g., publicly funded legal representation, high caseloads, and time pressures) often place practical limits on use of expert testimony. In the authors' experiences, mental health professionals are likelier to be called to testify when termination of parental rights is at issue, in high-profile or highly contested cases, or when private attorneys are involved.

This chapter covers issues in communicating FMHA results in child protection cases: including differences in reports written for therapeutic versus forensic consumers, strategies for organizing and writing forensic reports, and considerations in providing consultation and effective oral testimony. Although many aspects of reports and testimony apply across all forensic areas, this chapter highlights specific considerations in reporting on parenting capacity evaluations in child protection. Forensic parent evaluations, whether communicated in written or in oral form, can have a substantial impact on court decisions (Budd, 2005). Well organized, clear communication of forensic data can be helpful or even pivotal to legal consumers, but poorly presented information can obscure or confuse the judicial process. As Melton and colleagues (Melton et al., 2007, p. 578) stated, "above all, [forensic] *clinicians should be effective advocates for their data* [emphasis in original], whether or not that makes them effective advocates for the party that calls them to court."

Reports Written for Clinical Versus Forensic Consumers

Writing effective mental health reports requires careful selection, organization, and synthesis of a large volume of information (Sattler, 1998). Although the skills of clear communication are necessary to all types of reports, forensic reports differ in several important ways from clinical or therapeutic reports (Heilbrun, 2001; Heilbrun, Grisso, & Goldstein, 2009; Melton et al., 2007; also refer to Chapter 2 of this volume). The first difference is that the main consumers of therapeutic evaluations are mental health professionals and their patients, who are interested in issues of diagnosis and treatment. In contrast, the primary consumers of forensic evaluations are attorneys, judges, caseworkers, and laypersons interested in psycholegal issues. Clinical terms that may be useful for communicating information to therapeutic consumers are likely to be confusing to recipients of forensic reports. In a study conducted by Petrella and Poythress (1979, cited in Melton et al., 2007, p. 586), judges and lawyers labeled as "unclear" numerous terms found in forensic reports, including the following: *delusional ideation; affect; neologisms; loosening of associations; flight of ideas; blocking; oriented to time, place, and person; lability; flat affect; grandiosity; personality deficit; hysterical amnesia;* and *psychotic mentation.*

Evaluators are likely to be more helpful to the court by describing findings in behavioral terms rather than by invoking professional jargon. Likewise, use of diagnostic labels such as *obsessive compulsive* or *borderline*, without explanation, may connote unexpected and even incorrect information to the court. Legal consumers may assign the generally accepted meaning of diagnostic phrases (e.g., the belief that *schizophrenia* means "split personality") rather than the professional meaning (Melton et al., 2007, p. 586). If referencing a technical term that cannot be avoided (e.g., *mental health diagnosis, psychological test,* or *psychotropic medication*), offering a definition for the term via a footnote creates a more user-friendly document. When there is reason to use psychological terms or constructs in forensic reports, it is incumbent on the MHP to provide descriptive information to clarify the meaning and relevance. The terms *attachment* and *bonding*, for example, have quite different meanings in child developmental literature than may be understood by laypersons. In parent and adoptive contexts, "attachment" is used by laypersons not to describe a child's behavior and affect specific to a caregiver, but as an explanation for almost any behavioral symptoms or problems associated with the foster or adoption process (Nilsen, 2003). Similarly, laypersons often refer to an adolescent as having "bonded" with foster parents after a few months of placement. The use of the term *defensive* to describe a test-taker's efforts at impression management may conjure up an argumentative, oppositional character; or the use of the term *denied* to describe a parent's response to a particular question (e.g., "The mother denied a history of substance abuse") can convey that you do not believe this to be accurate.

A second difference between forensic and therapeutic reports relates to the compulsory nature of the FMHA. Unlike therapeutic assessments, forensic assessments of parents in child protection are generally compelled. Thus, the MHP undertakes a number of steps (as described in Chapter 5) beginning at the outset of the assessment to communicate these differences to all assessed parties and ensure their understanding. In the report, the MHP should explicitly document the methods used to provide the notification of purpose (or, in voluntary evaluations, informed consent) and the limits of confidentiality. A similar notice should be provided to collateral parties. In contrast to the privacy afforded persons in therapeutic evaluations, the substance of a forensic examinee's communications and test data is more likely to become public knowledge through media,

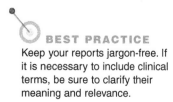

BEST PRACTICE
Keep your reports jargon-free. If it is necessary to include clinical terms, be sure to clarify their meaning and relevance.

7
chapter

court records, or persons observing court proceedings (Melton et al., 2007).

A third difference between forensic and therapeutic assessment reports is the context in which evaluations are performed. Therapeutic evaluations typically occur in a collaborative professional environment, with no expectation of any challenge to either the process or the conclusion. In contrast, forensic evaluations are performed within an adversarial legal environment that anticipates challenges of data, procedures, and conclusions through use of the rules of evidence. In order to prepare a report that will withstand close scrutiny during adversarial proceedings, the MHP must provide detailed information on the process of the evaluation, the data collected, the conclusions derived, and the nexus between that data and the evaluator's conclusions. Recommended methods of accomplishing these objectives are discussed next.

Strategies for Organizing and Writing Child Protection Reports

Considering the high volume of assessment reports prepared for the court and their importance in legal decisions, it is surprising that no specific standards exist for what constitutes an acceptable forensic report. In the absence of accepted standards, scholars have provided general guidelines. Heilbrun (2001) articulated three principles relevant to communication of FMHA results: (1) attribute information to specific sources; (2) use plain language and avoid technical jargon; and (3) write the report in sections, use a model, and employ procedures to cross-check facts and clarify the relationship between data, reasoning, and conclusions. For example, in one clearly labeled section the report could contain a summary of what was documented in prior records before the evaluation began. A separate section might contain the background as reported by the examinee. Another section might address information garnered from third-party sources about the same issues. The evaluator might then synthesize all of these data and, combined with the evaluator's own observations, summarize what is known, what is controverted, and what can be concluded from the data. In this way the reader can understand the sources for each assumption, and there is little danger of misattributing data.

Melton et al. (2007, pp. 583-586) discussed four general recommendations for writing reports consistent with Heilbrun's (2001) principles. In addition to suggestions regarding organization and careful data documentation, Melton and colleagues offered some direction regarding the content of the report. Their recommendations were to:

(1) Separate facts from inferences (i.e., present facts and descriptive material separately from theoretical and clinical inferences, and link the clinical data to the legal referral questions);

(2) Stay within the scope of the referral question (i.e., by confining the report to topics raised by the referral source and avoiding inclusion of irrelevant issues, even if the topics would be relevant in a therapeutic evaluation context);

(3) Avoid information over- (and under-) kill (i.e., strike a balance between comprehensiveness and efficiency by reporting findings essential to the clinical formulation); and

(4) Minimize clinical jargon (as described previously).

"Staying within the scope" might mean, for example, that a parent's remote history of arrest for driving while intoxicated would be omitted when there is no reason to suspect current alcohol abuse, or another parent's civil action in a workplace-harassment matter would have no bearing on the current evaluation.

The process of preparing an effective forensic report begins with organizing and interpreting the data collected, as described in Chapter 6, followed by distilling the essential material into a

7
chapter

written document. The MHP must make some decisions about what information to include, keeping in mind what information will be most relevant to the consumers of the findings. Through the report-writing task, evaluators are required to impose some order on their gathered data; address alternative hypotheses; identify the limitations of the available data; and, anticipating close legal scrutiny, scientifically defend their documented conclusions. These are essentially independent judgments of the MHP, although they may be influenced by consultation with legal or clinical colleagues or by prevailing practices of the forensic setting. To illustrate: An evaluator may collect data spanning 15 years of child protection services with a parent including mental health treatment records from several therapists. For the purposes of the current assessment, the salient data extracted from these documents might be described in two or three paragraphs summarizing the general thrust of the intervention, benefits apparently derived, and obstacles that might have prevented further benefit. Detailing the date and nature of each intervention, the number of therapy sessions, or the summaries of each individual intervention, while useful in some other contexts, would probably lead to creating a report too lengthy and comprehensive to be practically useful for the current purposes. Documentation of the specific reports used in compiling such a summary is, however, essential.

The organization of the forensic report should proceed from data, to inferences, to conclusions (Melton et al., 2007). Ordinarily a forensic report includes the following topics: identifying data regarding the subject(s) of the report; referral information and the legal basis for the evaluation; techniques utilized for assessment; description of the notification of purpose (or informed consent) and limitation-of-confidentiality discussion with the examinee(s); description of the data collected; and analysis of the data, conclusions, and recommendations, with the findings or opinions clearly linking the data to the purpose for which the evaluation was undertaken and the opinions that resulted. Because judges and attorneys are accustomed to scanning cases and briefs to look for legal issues most pertinent to their arguments, forensic evaluators have developed a style that facilitates this approach through the use of topical headings that identify different types of information.

The length of forensic reports varies considerably across cases, MHPs, and forensic settings, from as short as two pages

to upwards of 100 pages. Although there are no formal guidelines for the length of reports, evaluators should keep in mind their audience in determining how much information is likely to be read and what is essential to documenting the assessment process and results. As the length of reports increases, the importance of section titles and evaluation summaries increases because consumers are less likely to read the entire document. Some authors (Melton et al., 2007; Pezzot-Pearce & Pearce, 2004) have suggested including supporting data or references in an addendum when needed; however, this practice can add substantially to the length of the document and may not enhance communication. If an addendum is used, the materials should be clearly introduced in the body of the report, and the rationale for their inclusion should be stated.

Writing for a Child Protection Audience

The audience for child protection evaluations is multidisciplinary and may include the court, attorneys, caseworkers, therapists, parent trainers, and the parents themselves. (Although many evaluators do not routinely provide parents with a copy of the report, parents who represent themselves in court are required by law to have access, and others may obtain a copy from their attorneys.) The range of sophistication among readers is broad, and those most in need of a clear understanding of the findings may have very limited understanding of how those findings were derived. The reader may have limited understanding of what psychological tests can and cannot do, the implications of limited confidentiality, or how the parent's attitude toward the evaluation may influence the findings. Technical language describing such phenomena as test reliability or clinical diagnoses may be unintelligible to readers.

7
chapter

Whether the evaluator provides feedback directly to the examinee or leaves that task to attorneys, caseworkers, and therapists, the evaluator should bear in mind that the results may be devastating or confusing to the parent. Care should be taken in the report and in testimony to communicate in language that can be understood and to explain how circumstances evolved to produce the results found. Rather than saying the parent is so depressed that this emotional state may compromise adequate parenting, for example, the etiology of the depression might be described—the losses and difficulties faced by the parent that underlie the depression; the parent's efforts to deal with it through "self-medication," avoidance, or withdrawal; and the net effect, not just on the child, but on the parent who may feel isolated and hopeless in the face of the current stressors.

The general forensic report guidelines just described apply to parenting capacity evaluations in child protection cases. In addition, several features have been recommended specifically for parent evaluations (Budd, 2001; Pezzot-Pearce & Pearce, 2004). In their examination of parent evaluations conducted in an urban juvenile court system, Budd and colleagues described specific features recommended in the forensic literature that were frequently missing in child protection reports (Budd et al., 2001). These include a listing of specific referral questions and the response to each question as part of the clinical summary; statement of the statutory issue or legal options under consideration; and description of the notification of purpose and limits of confidentiality. In reporting results, Budd and colleagues found that parent evaluations often emphasized parental weaknesses over parental strengths, and they rarely included information on parents' caregiving skills or on the child's relationship with the parent.

One example of an organizing format for evaluations of parents in child protection cases is provided in Table 7.1. This format is adapted from the court-based clinic model used in

BEST PRACTICE
In addition to adhering to general forensic report guidelines, child protection reports should include a list of referral questions with responses, a statement of the legal issue at hand, and a description of how informed consent was provided.

Table 7.1 Outline of Report of Parenting Capacity Evaluation (from Budd, 2001)

1.   Identifying information
2.   Reason for referral
3.   Summary of assessment contacts and activities by date
4.   Assessment measures administered
5.   Records reviewed
6.   Information from relevant records
7.   Notification of purpose and warning of limits on confidentiality
8.   Behavioral observations and mental status
9.   Information from clinical and collateral interviews
10. Results of tests
11. Observation of parent–child interactions
12. Clinical summary
13. Summary of recommendations
14. Dated signature and credentials

the Cook County Juvenile Court system (Budd et al., 2006, as described in Chapter 3). Further information regarding the recommended content for each section is provided in Budd (2001). Samples of assessment reports on parents in child protection cases are available as models (Melton et al., 2007; Oberlander, 2002; Pezzot-Pearce & Pearce, 2004).

Considerations in Providing Consultation and Effective Oral Testimony

Effective oral testimony is based on both substantive and stylistic aspects (Heilbrun, 2001). The substantive part of expert testimony is addressed by quality of the forensic evaluation and written report, whereas the stylistic aspect concerns how the expert presents, speaks, and otherwise behaves to make her testimony more understandable and credible. For maximum effectiveness, both the substance and style of the expert testimony should be strong. Although both aspects are important, testimony that is substantively weak but stylistically impressive should be identified and accorded little weight, if forensic mental health professionals are to contribute meaningfully to legal decision making. Conversely, testimony that is substantively strong but stylistically weak may have little influence or may be misunderstood. MHPs need to have both substantive and stylistic skill sets to testify effectively (Heilbrun & Goldstein, 2009).

Several forensic resources provide useful commentaries on issues and strategies for effective oral communication (Brodsky, 1991, 1999, 2004, 2009; Heilbrun, 2001). The following sections discuss the application of these skills to evaluations of parenting capacity in a child protection context. Because little has been written on oral communication in this particular context, the material relies heavily on experiences of the authors.

Informal Communication

Oral communication regarding child protection evaluation results may be informal (e.g., feedback to caseworkers and attorneys) or formal (testimony in a deposition, hearing, or trial). Although written reports embody all of the evaluator's opinions resulting from the data available at the time of the assessments and provide the parties a good idea of what the expert would say during testimony, it is not possible to cross-examine a report. The attorneys for the parent, for example, may seek further information, either through consultation, deposition, or testimony. Informal communication through consultation with the parents' attorneys should be approached with caution, particularly if it occurs *ex parte* or with only one side. Evaluators may choose to avoid such communications or to insist that both the parents' attorney and the attorney for the state be present for informal consultation to avoid appearance of collusion with one side or the other. It is particularly important to be sure that the party least favored by the findings has equal access to the evaluator.

BEWARE When meeting with attorneys, include both sides or offer each side equal time.

Should informal consultation occur, the evaluator remains neutral about any settlement aims. When parties or their counsel provide new information about issues addressed in the report or when a parent's circumstances change, this information should be noted and any changes in the evaluator's recommendations should be documented as well. Great caution is in order in making such amendments based on informal consultation. The contextual pressures and the absence of time to reflectively consider the new information, its sources, and the presence or absence of corroborative support all argue for taking time to consider the new information. Documentation should be sought for new information if it forms the basis for further consideration. Failing to attend to these issues creates the risk of ill-considered comments from the evaluator. A good approach might be to invite the party with new information to reiterate it in writing and allow time for the evaluator to consider what, if any, impact the new information may have on his recommendations and if additional data need to be collected to form a conclusion. For example, a parent's attorney may report that since the completion of the evaluation, the parent has moved into more suitable housing or obtained stable employment, or has begun a serious course of intervention to address her drug addiction. This new information might merit further consideration if the issues addressed were fundamental to the evaluator's findings and recommendations.

Deposition

Informal consultations with counsel may sometimes occur in child protection matters, but depositions are far less frequent, for several reasons. Counsel for parents may be working with restrictive budgets and may not be able to undertake the expense of depositions, which involve hourly fees and court-reporter or videographer fees. The expense, therefore, often precludes deposition as a source of pretrial discovery. Depositions also involve advance planning and, if counsel is obtained just before trial, there may not be time for such discovery. Furthermore, without the assistance of a mental health expert, the parent's counsel may be reluctant to attempt to probe the bases for the evaluator's findings. Evaluators may be unable to schedule deposition time on short notice as well. In preparation for responding to the request for deposition or affidavit of expected testimony, the evaluator may find it useful to consult general forensic texts for available options (Brodsky, 1991, 1999, 2004; Haller, 2002; Heilbrun, 2001).

Expert Testimony

Court testimony is required in some cases, but it may occur more or less frequently depending on the jurisdiction. Compared to child custody, criminal, and general civil cases, child protection cases often allow for little pretrial preparation, and the evaluator may have little foreknowledge about what will be asked, what points are likely to be pursued on cross-examination, or how knowledgeably the attorneys might approach expert psychological testimony. Evaluators should attempt, whenever possible, to engage in pretrial preparation with the attorney who has issued the subpoena. Not only does this provide the evaluator with specific information about questions that will be posed, but it allows her to assist the attorney in wording questions in a way that will elicit the most useful and relevant information. It is useful to prepare for challenges to the admissibility of the testimony and to assume those present for the testimony have little or no understanding of psychological assessment techniques. Although some counsel and judges may be experienced in dealing with mental health expertise in child protection matters, others, and of course the parents, will benefit from clear explanations free of professional jargon.

To prepare for challenges to the admissibility of expert testimony, the evaluator should review the psychometric properties of each instrument employed, including the standardization population, reliability, validity, and relevance to or appropriateness of its use in the current

evaluation (Krauss & Sales, 2003). Buros Institute of Mental Measurements (2009) provides online access to professional reviews of instruments commonly recognized for psychological evaluations. Furthermore, it is important to become familiar with the professional community's opinions about any instrument (available in peer-reviewed articles). Some instruments may be well accepted for some circumstances but controversial or outright inappropriate for parenting assessment. For example, the Rorschach may enjoy general acceptance for use in clinical settings (see, for example, Meyer & Archer, 2001; and Weiner, 1999; but also see Hunsley & Bailey, 1999), but its use in forensic settings sparks considerable controversy (see, for example, Wood et al., 2001). Similarly, use of the Child Abuse Potential Inventory may be easily defended in a case involving alleged physical abuse of a young child by parents of lower socioeconomic circumstances, but it would be inappropriate for use when child sexual abuse is the primary focus of the evaluation (Milner, 2004). The evaluator using the CAPI might face a challenge regarding the instrument's predictive validity, in light of research showing a high rate of false positives for parents scoring above the clinical cutoff on the Abuse scale. Despite a significant correlation between Abuse scale scores and subsequent confirmed child abuse, the majority of parents earning elevated abuse scores did not later abuse their children (Milner et al., 1984).

The forensic evaluator may be asked to indicate how important the testing was to the overall opinions being offered and also with what degree of psychological certainty she holds those opinions. Psychologists are generally not trained to quantify opinions in this way, and they should not attempt to create answers just to be helpful. It is acceptable to use qualitative answers or to decline to give percentages when to do so would be baseless and therefore potentially misleading. To be helpful to the fact finder, the evaluator may offer an explanation that embraces the spirit of the question, such as, "I considered the test results along with all of the other data, including interviews, document review, and collateral interviews, and formed my opinions based on all of the information. Without test data, I might have failed to appreciate how

[Ms. X's depression affected her ability to manage the demands of parenting] [Mr. X's cognitive limitations affected his capacity to hold a job, his understanding of his child's ADHD condition, and his ability to benefit from insight-oriented psychotherapy]. However, I cannot say that my opinions would have been altogether different without the test results or that test data accounted for a certain percentage of my opinion." Regarding the degree of psychological certainty with which an opinion is held, a similarly qualitative response may be sufficient. For example, the evaluator might describe his certainty in terms such as "reasonably confident" or "slightly more likely than not" and point out the factors that could cause his opinion to be wrong.

Once any evidentiary issues or challenges to admissibility of testimony have been resolved, the evaluator's testimony is then given. Even though the court may be familiar with the evaluator's qualifications, it is common for the party offering her testimony (generally the party most favored by the report) to begin the direct examination by asking the evaluator to review those qualifications and then to offer her curriculum vitae into evidence. The opposing party may have some questions about those credentials, such as how many times the evaluator has done an assessment of a family of the ethnicity or religion of the parties, how many times the evaluator has testified on behalf of parents in such proceedings, whether the evaluator has ever had a professional licensing board complaint, or any number of

INFO

Common questions during direct examination testimony in child protection:

1. What were you asked to do in this case?

2. What techniques did you employ?

3. What were the findings from each of those techniques?

4. How did you pull this information together? (hypothesis generation, assimilation of data, distilling opinions in an explicit way that accounts for what data supported and what data ran counter to each hypothesis, formulation of final opinions)

5. What opinion do you hold?

other issues. These questions often are intended to cast doubt on the evaluator's qualifications as an expert. Following this questioning, which may involve several rounds of redirect and recross, the court then rules on the evaluator's qualifications as an expert for the purposes offered.

The direct examination proceeds generally along a line of questions, as exemplified in the adjacent information box. The same suggestions hold true for testimony as for report writing; that is, proceed by describing evaluation techniques, the data those techniques have produced, inferences drawn from the data, and the conclusions. It is crucial that the evaluator know the case well enough to answer questions conversationally rather than to rifle through files searching for information. Details the MHP should have readily available include the nature and date of the initial contact with the referral source, and steps taken to gather data (e.g., dates of the interview and testing sessions with subjects and collaterals, length of time spent with each party, documents reviewed, tests administered, and any observations conducted). The attorney may interject questions to ask about the results of each test, what was gleaned from each collateral contact, or other details.

INFO

Common techniques used in cross-examination of testimony in child protection:

1. Attack the evaluator's knowledge or experience

2. Search for bias or premature opinion formulation

3. Attack the basis for the opinion ("How much time did you spend with my client?" "Did my client have the opportunity to challenge the bases for your opinion?" "On what information did you base your opinion that the parent is able to parent adequately?")

4. Attack the techniques ("How are these tests constructed?" "How do you interpret them?" "What do they have to do with adequate parenting?")

5. Convert evaluator to one's own expert ("What were some of my client's strengths?" "Were there some good reasons my client could not participate in all of the elements of the casework plan?" "What risk factors are present in this case for future abuse or neglect?")

The forensic report serves as an outline so the attorney knows what information the testimony can encompass. The attorney will often ask specific questions drawn from the information in the report to elicit testimony about particularly salient aspects of the case.

The cross-examination may proceed along any one of several lines, depending on the attorney's style and the points upon which the evaluation results can be challenged. A well-prepared attorney will have consulted a psychologist to help develop good cross-examination strategies. Whatever line is taken, the evaluator must remember that the attorney is zealously advocating the interests of the client, and the line of questioning is not a personal assault.

The evaluator should strive to answer cross-examination questions with the same demeanor and attitude he employed on direct examination. This may be difficult when an attorney's approach is particularly gruff or accusatory, but the evaluator who becomes defensive or angry loses credibility.

Sometimes it is difficult or impossible to answer a yes or no question without further elaboration. For example, if asked if the findings of the evaluation supported a conclusion that the parent was unable to understand the child's developmental capacities, the evaluator might find that neither a straightforward yes or no answer accurately describes the findings. Rather, the findings might suggest some impairment in the parent's understanding of the child's developmental capacities, but a clear capacity and motivation to learn. In another instance, an evaluator might be asked if the parent was cooperative with the evaluation process. The parent may have shown some evidence of cooperation, by keeping appointments and completing pencil and paper testing, but she may have given highly defensive or minimal responses during interviews, asserting that the information sought had nothing to do with the issues at hand. When it is not possible to give a yes or no answer, the evaluator may explain that a yes or no answer would be misleading or cannot be given, and offer an explanation. The attorney may insist on a yes or no answer and the court may intervene, either directing the forensic evaluator to answer or allowing an explanation. Any obfuscation of the data that occurs during cross-examination may be cleared up on redirect; it is helpful to the process and ensures that testimony is accurate if the examiner indicates the need to explain. The attorney conducting cross-examination may not provide that opportunity, but the other attorney is likely to make a note of it and provide the forensic expert with the opportunity on redirect.

Evaluators may be faced with poorly worded or confusing questions on the stand; sometimes intentional and sometimes not. First, it is important before answering any question to allow time for the opposing counsel to object. If a question is poorly worded or confusing, often the objection process will lead to a resolution. Should this not occur, or if the objection is overruled, the evaluator should indicate that he needs clarification prior to providing an answer. Another approach is to reply in a manner that addresses the confusing nature of the question. For example, if asked, "Would you be surprised to know that the mother has complied with all services since you completed your evaluation?" the evaluator, if given the latitude to provide more than a yes or no reply, could explain that she would not have any particular emotional reaction to this information, but that this information is not consistent with the parent's previous behavior.

Evaluators may also be faced with hypothetical questions or be asked to speculate about the future (e.g., "If you knew that the mother had participated in all visits since you completed your evaluation, would this change your opinion?"). It is important in these situations to apply the same interpretive principles as discussed in Chapter 6: that conclusions should not be drawn based on a single datum. In such situations, it is appropriate for the evaluator to explain that additional steps would need to be taken, not only to confirm the validity of the information but to gather other relevant data prior to making a statement about how it might change his opinion or conclusion.

Regardless of which side calls the MHP to testify, the evaluator's obligation is to provide objective, reliable data on which the fact finder can rely. In most situations, data can be found to support both the evaluator's opinions and countervailing opinions. The MHP has a professional obligation to testify truthfully and to take an affirmative role in being sure that her testimony fairly represents the data. Yet, testimony is elicited in a question-and-answer format, such that volunteering information may not be looked upon favorably. The forensic evaluator may address this problem by providing a preface to her answers throughout testimony but particularly at the point of offering final opinions or recommendations. For example, the evaluator could make a comment such as "There were both positive and negative factors..." or "Ms. X's evaluation results included both strengths and areas of concern...." This cues Ms. X's attorney to draw out the strengths, and the opposing attorney to elicit the areas of concern.

Summary

The evaluation of parents in a child protection matter concludes with the presentation of the evaluation results to those concerned with disposition of the case. That may include the parties and their counsel, child welfare and mental health service providers, and the court. Results are invariably presented in the form of written reports and may also be presented through testimony, either by deposition or in court. Because forensic report writing is different in significant ways from clinical report writing, strategies for organizing and writing forensic reports in this context require special skills. Sound reports and testimony describe why the evaluation was initiated, how it was structured, what was found, how reliable those findings can be considered to be, the nexus between the data and the opinions, and what relevance the findings may have to the matter before the court. In addition to substantive skills, effective testimony requires stylistic skills in preparing and presenting information in the adversarial context of the courtroom.

The findings and recommendations of a parenting capacity evaluation may serve multiple functions. The report may assist caseworkers in planning, treatment providers in crafting and carrying out treatment plans, attorneys and the parties in determining how they wish to proceed, and the court in understanding psychological issues relevant to legal decision making. In this way, the report is often far more broadly useful than the reports prepared in some other kinds of forensic evaluations when the psycholegal question is quite narrow, such as competency to stand trial or criminal responsibility, or when the report is utilized for a narrow purpose, such as a presentencing report or a report of the assessment of a juvenile's capacity to be tried as an adult.

Given this potentially broad use of the parenting evaluation in child protection matters, it is helpful to keep in mind that the report may be read by people with widely varying levels of understanding of the facts of the case, the history of the person being evaluated, and the implications of these findings within the child protection system. Furthermore, the report may "follow" the examinee through many years of intervention and continue to have a powerful impact on perceptions of others. For these reasons, it is essential that the findings be described in language free of disparagement and that both parental strengths and areas needing intervention be fully described. Conclusions should be offered with the caution appropriate to an evolving story, recognizing that subsequent events may alter or contradict any opinions or predictions.

This volume has discussed issues and methods in FMHA of parents and the parent–child relationship in child protection matters. Two competing tensions—the right to parent, and society's responsibility to protect its children—converge and, at times, collide in child protection proceedings. Parenting capacity evaluations present

BEST PRACTICE

Parent-evaluation reports may be read by individuals with varying levels of understanding of the facts of the case, the history of the evaluee, and the implications of the report's findings. Be sure to use impartial language and report equally on parental strengths and weaknesses.

7
chapter

unique challenges from the initial referral to the final summary of findings, owing to numerous factors specific to child protection cases. These factors include definitional vagueness of what constitutes minimal parenting adequacy; multiple and complicated factors affecting parenting, parent–child relationships, and child outcomes; the relatively recent history of forensic parent assessment practices in child protection and the small research base relevant to this context; and the pressures evaluators often face in managing a high volume of child protection referrals in a timely way.

Conducting sound parent evaluations requires solid clinical and forensic skills as well as knowledge of child development, parenting, and the child welfare system. Most MHPs come to this work with a background in only some of these areas, fueling the need for continuing education and training. Despite its challenges, the work carries important consequences and rewards in that a well-constructed, balanced evaluation can have a pivotal impact on child protection decisions. By applying current best practices in planning and conducting parenting capacity evaluations, MHPs can contribute valuable information on complicated issues affecting the safety and well-being of children and families.

References

Abidin, R., Flens, J. R., & Austin, W. G. (2006). The Parenting Stress Index. In R. P. Archer (Ed.), *Forensic uses of clinical assessment instruments* (pp. 297–328). Mahwah, NJ: Lawrence Erlbaum Associates, Publishers.

Administrative Office of the Courts, American Institutes for Research. (2002) *Unified family court evaluation literature review*. Contract Number 1001959. Retrieved October 27, 2010 from http://www.courtinfo.ca.gov/programs/cfcc/pdffiles/ufclitreview.pdf

Adoption and Safe Families Act of 1997. Pub. L. No. 105-89. 42 U.S.C. 675.

Adoption Assistance and Child Welfare Act of 1980. P.L. 96-272, 42 U.S.C.

Ainsworth, M. D., Blehar, M., Waters, E., & Wall, S. (1978). *Patterns of attachment*. Hillsdale, NJ: Lawrence Erlbaum.

American Academy of Child & Adolescent Psychiatry (AACAP) (1990). *Guidelines for the clinical evaluation for child and adolescent sexual abuse. Position statement of the American Academy of Child and Adolescent Psychiatry*. Retrieved May 11, 2008, from http://www.aacap.org/cs/root/policy_statements/guidelines_for_the_clinical_evaluation_for_child_and_adolescent_sexual_abuse

American Educational Research Association, American Psychological Association, & National Council on Measurement in Education (1999). *Standards for educational and psychological testing*. Washington, D.C.: AERA (published by American Educational Research Association).

American Humane Society (n.d.). The real story of Mary Ellen Wilson. Retrieved June 7, 2008, from the American Humane Society Web page: http://www.americanhumane.org/site/PageServer?pagename=wh_mission_maryellen.

American Professional Society on the Abuse of Children (APSAC) (1995). *Use of anatomical dolls in child sexual abuse assessments*. Chicago, IL: APSAC.

APSAC Task Force on the Psychosocial Evaluation of Suspected Sexual Abuse in Children (1990; 1997; 2002). *Psychosocial evaluation of suspected sexual abuse in children* (2nd ed.). Chicago, IL: APSAC.

American Psychological Association (APA) (1995). *Questions and answers about memories of childhood abuse*. Retrieved February 18, 2008, from http://www.apa.org/topics/memories.html.

APA (2002). Ethical principles of psychologists and code of conduct. *American Psychologist, 57*, 1060–1073.

APA (2007). Record keeping guidelines. *American Psychologist, 62*, 993–1004.

APA Committee on Professional Practice and Standards (1999). Guidelines for psychological evaluations in child protection matters. *American Psychologist, 54*, 586–593.

American Psychological Association. (2009). Effective strategies to support positive parenting in community health centers: Report of the Working Group on Child Maltreatment Prevention in Community Health Centers: Washington, DC: Author.

Annie M. Case Foundation (2009). *Issue brief: Rebuild the nation's child welfare system*. Retrieved on March 12, 2009, from http://www.aecf.org//media/PublicationFiles/Child_Welfare_issuebrief2.pdf.

Archer, R. P., Buffington-Vollum, J. K., Stredny, R. V., & Handel, R. W. (2006). A survey of psychological test use patterns among forensic psychologists. *Journal of Personality Assessment, 87*, 84–94.

Arnold, D. S., O'Leary, S. G., Wolff, L. S., & Acker, M. M. (1993). The Parenting Scale: A measure of dysfunctional parenting in discipline situations. *Psychological Assessment, 5*, 137–144.

Aucion, K. J., Frick, P. J., & Bodin, S. D. (2006). Corporal punishment and child adjustment. *Journal of Applied Developmental Psychology, 27*, 527–541.

Azar, S. T., & Benjet, C. L. (1994). A cognitive perspective on ethnicity, race, and termination of parental rights. *Law and Human Behavior, 18*, 249–268.

Azar, S. T., Benjet, C. L., Fuhrmann, G. S., & Cavellero, L. (1995). Child maltreatment and termination of parental rights: Can behavioral research help Solomon? *Behavior Therapy, 26*, 599–623.

Azar, S. T., & Goff, P. A. (2007). Can science help Solomon? Child maltreatment cases and the potential for racial and ethnic bias in decision making. *Saint John's Law Review, 81*, 533–573.

Azar, S. T., Lauretti, A. F., & Loding, B. V. (1998). The evaluation of parental fitness in termination of parental rights cases: A functional-contextual perspective. *Clinical* Child and Family Psychology Review, *1*, 77–100.

Azar, S. T., Robinson, D. R., Hekimian, E., & Twentyman, C. T. (1984). Unrealistic expectations and problem-solving ability in maltreating and comparison mothers. *Journal of Consulting and Clinical Psychology, 52*, 687–691.

Azar, S. T., & Rohrbeck, C. A. (1986). Child abuse and unrealistic expectations: Further validation of the Parent Opinion Questionnaire. *Journal of Consulting and Clinical Psychology, 54*, 867–868.

Babb, B. A. (2008). Reevaluating where we stand: A comprehensive survey of America's Family Justice Systems. *Family Court Review, 46*, 230–257.

Badeau, S., & Gesiriech, S. (2003). *A child's journey through the child welfare system*. Retrieved November 19, 2008, from Pew Commission on Children in Foster Care Web site: http://pewfostercare.org/docs/index.php?DocID=24.

Baerger, D. R., & Budd, K. S. (2003). Parental competency to consent in child protection proceedings. *Family Law Psychology Briefs, 4*. Retrieved from http://www.jmcraig.com/subscribers/archives.htm.

Barber, B. K. (1996). Parental psychological control: Revisiting a neglected construct. *Child Development, 67*, 3296–3319.

Barber, B. K. (Ed.) (2002). *Intrusive parenting: How psychological control affects children and adolescents.* Washington, D.C.: American Psychological Association.

Barnum, R. (1997). A suggested framework for forensic consultation in cases of child abuse and neglect. *Journal of the American Academy of Psychiatry and the Law, 25,* 581–593.

Barnum, R. (2002). Parenting assessment in cases of neglect and abuse. In D. H. Schetky & E. P. Benedek (Eds.), *Principles and practice of child and adolescent forensic psychiatry* (pp. 81–96). Arlington, VA: American Psychiatric Publishing.

Baumrind, D. (1971). Current patterns of parental authority. *Developmental Psychology Monographs, 4,* 1–103.

Baumrind, D. (1991). Parenting styles and adolescent development. In J. Brooks-Gunn, R. Lerner, & A. C. Peterson (Eds.), *The encyclopedia of adolescence* (pp. 746–758). New York: Garland.

Baumrind, D. (1995). *Child maltreatment and optimal caregiving in social contexts.* New York: Garland Publishing.

Bavolek, S. J. (1984). *Handbook of the AAPI—Adult-Adolescent Parenting Inventory.* Eau Claire, WI: Family Development Resources.

Bavolek, S., J., & Keene, R. G. (1999). *Adult-Adolescent Parenting Inventory—AAPI-2: Administration and development handbook.* Park City, UT: Family Development Resources.

Belsky, J. (1993). Etiology of child maltreatment: A developmental-ecological analysis. *Psychological Bulletin, 114,* 413–434.

Benjet, C., Azar, S. T., & Kuersten-Hogan, R. (2003). Evaluating the parental fitness of psychiatrically diagnosed individuals: Advocating a functional-contextual analysis of parenting. *Journal of Family Psychology, 17,* 238–251.

Ben-Porath, Y. S. (2009). *The MMPI-2-RF (Restructured Form): An introduction for forensic psychologists.* Workshop presented at the American Academy of Forensic Psychology, March 2009, Montreal, Q.C.

Ben-Porath, Y. S., & Tellegen, A. (2008). *MMPI-2-RF (Minnesota Multiphasic Personality Inventory-2): Manual for administration, scoring, and interpretation.* Minneapolis: University of Minnesota Press.

Berk, L. E. (2008). *Infants and children: Prenatal through middle childhood* (6th ed.). Boston: Pearson Education.

Beyer, M. (1993). *What do children and families need?* Paper presented at the American Bar Association conference: Children and the Law, June 1993, Washington, D.C.

Bishop, S. J., Murphy, J. M., Hicks, R., Quinn, D., Lewis, P. J., Grace, M., & Jellinek, M. S., (2003). What progress has been made in meeting the needs of seriously maltreated children? The course of 200 cases through the Boston Juvenile Court. *Child Abuse & Neglect, 24,* 599–610.

Boothroyd, R. A. (2004). Review of the Parent-Child Relationship Inventory. *Mental Measurements Yearbook, 13* (accession no. 13121821).

Bornstein, M. H. (Ed.) (2002). *Handbook of parenting (vols. 1–4).* Mahwah, NJ: Lawrence Erlbaum Associates, Publishers.

Bowlby, J. (1969/1982). *Attachment and loss, Vol. 1: Attachment.* New York: Basic Books.

Brodsky, S. L. (1991). *Testifying in court: Guidelines and maxims for the expert witness.* Washington, D.C.: American Psychological Association.

Brodsky, S. L. (1999). *The expert expert witness: More maxims and guidelines for testifying in court.* Washington, D.C.: American Psychological Association.

Brodsky, S. L. (2004). *Coping with cross-examination and other pathways to effective testimony.* Washington, D.C.: American Psychological Association.

Brodsky, S. L. (2009). *Principles and practice of trial consultation.* New York: Guilford Press.

Bronfenbrenner, U. (1979). *The ecology of human development.* Cambridge, MA: Harvard University Press.

Brown, J., Cohen, P., Johnson, J. G., & Salzinger, S. (1998). A longitudinal analysis of risk factors for child maltreatment: Findings of a 17-year prospective study of officially recorded and self-reported child abuse and neglect. *Child Abuse & Neglect, 22,* 1065–1078.

Budd, K. S. (2001). Assessing parenting competence in child protection cases: A clinical practice model. *Clinical Child and Family Psychology Review, 4,* 1–18.

Budd, K. S. (2005). Assessing parenting capacity in a child welfare context. *Children and Youth Services Review, 27,* 429–444.

Budd, K. S., Felix, E. D., Poindexter, L. M., Naik-Polan, A. T., & Sloss, C. F. (2002). Clinical assessment of children in child protection cases: An empirical analysis. *Professional Psychology: Research and Practice, 33,* 3–12.

Budd, K. S., Felix, E. D., Sweet, S. C., Saul, A., & Carleton, R. A. (2006). Evaluating parents in child protection decisions: An innovative court-based clinic model. *Professional Psychology: Research and Practice, 37,* 666–675.

Budd, K. S., Heilman, N. E., & Kane, D. (2000). Psychosocial correlates of child abuse potential in multiple disadvantaged adolescent mothers. *Child Abuse & Neglect, 24,* 611–625.

Budd, K. S., & Holdsworth, M. J. (1996). Issues in clinical assessment of minimal parenting competence. *Journal of Clinical Child Psychology, 25,* 1–14.

Budd, K. S., Naik-Polan, A. T., Felix, E. D., Massey, L. P., & Eisele, H. (2004). Legal use of mental health evaluations in child protection proceedings: An empirical analysis. *Family Court Review, 42,* 629–640.

Budd, K. S., Poindexter, L. M., Felix, E. D., & Naik-Polan, A. T. (2001). Clinical assessment of parents in child protection cases: An empirical analysis. *Law and Human Behavior, 25,* 93–108.

Budd, K. S., & Springman, R. E. (in press). Empirical analysis of referral issues and "ultimate issue" recommendations for parents in child protection cases. *Family Court Review*.

Burns, B. J., Phillips, S. D., Wagner, R., Barth, R. P., Kolko, D. J., Campbell, Y., & Landsverk, J. (2004). Mental health need and access to mental health services by youth involved in child welfare: A national survey. *Journal of the American Academy of Child & Adolescent Psychiatry, 43*, 960–970.

Buros Institute of Mental Measurements (2009). *Test Reviews Online.* Retrieved June 7, 2009, at http://buros.unl.edu/buros/jsp/lists.jsp.

California Welf. & Inst. Code §§ 361.5; 366.26.

Carr, G. D., Moretti, M. M., & Cue, B. J. H. (2005). Evaluating parenting capacity: Validity problems with the MMPI-2, PAI, CAPI, and ratings of child adjustment. *Professional Psychology: Research and Practice, 36*, 188–196.

Cassidy, J., & Mohr, J. J. (2001). Unsolvable fear, trauma, and psychopathology: Theory, research, and clinical considerations related to disorganized attachment across the life span. *Clinical Psychology: Science and Practice, 8*, 275–298.

Cavanaugh, K., Dobash, R. E., & Dobash, R. P. (2007). The murder of children by fathers in the context of child abuse. *Child Abuse & Neglect, 31*, 731–746.

Center for Advanced Studies in Child Welfare, University of Minnesota (n.d.) *Termination of parental rights.* Retrieved November 2, 2008, from http://cehd.umn.edu/SSW/cascw/research/tpr/default.asp.

Center for the Study of Social Policy (2005). *Criteria and procedures for determining a "compelling reason" not to file a TPR: Discussion paper and approved recommendations.* Retrieved August 14, 2009, from http://www.cssp.org/uploadFiles/compellingReasons.pdf.

Chaffin, M., & Friedrich, B. (2004). Evidence-based treatments in child abuse and neglect. *Children and Youth Services Review, 26*, 1097–1113.

Chaffin, M., Silovsky, J. F., Funderburk, B., Valle, L., Brestan, E. V., Balachova, T., Jackson, S., Lensgraf, J., Bonner, B. L. (2004). Parent-child interaction therapy with physically abusive parents: Efficacy for reducing future abuse reports. *Journal of Consulting & Clinical Psychology, 72*, 500–510.

Chao, R. (1994). Beyond parental control and authoritarian parenting style: Understanding Chinese parenting through the cultural notion of training. *Child Development, 65*, 1111–1119.

Child Abuse Prevention and Treatment Act of 1974, Pub. L. No. 93-247.

Child Welfare Information Gateway (2006). *Court hearings for the permanent placement of children: Summary of state laws.* Retrieved November 2, 2008, from U.S. Department of Health and Human Services, Administration for Children and Families, Administration on Children, Youth, and Families, Children's Bureau website:

http://www.childwelfare.gov/systemwide/laws_policies/statutes/planningall.pdf.

Child Welfare Information Gateway (2007). *Grounds for involuntary termination of parental rights: State statutes series.* Retrieved November 2, 2008, from http://www.childwelfare.gov/systemwide/laws_policies/statutes/groundtermin.cfm.

Child Welfare Information Gateway (2008). *Determining the best interests of the child.* Retrieved from Child Welfare Information Gateway Web site March 15, 2009, at http://www.childwelfare.gov/systemwide/laws_policies/statutes/best_interest.cfm. Washington, D.C.: U.S. Department of Health and Human Services, Administration for Children and Families, Administration on Children, Youth, and Families, Children's Bureau, Office of Child Abuse and Neglect.

Cicchetti, D., Rogosch, F. A., & Toth, S. L. (2006). Fostering secure attachments in infants in maltreating families through preventive intervention. *Development and Psychopathology, 18,* 623–649.

Cohen, J. A., Mannarino, A. P., Murray, L. K., & Igelman, R. (2006). Psychosocial interventions for maltreated and violence-exposed children. *Journal of Social Issues, 62,* 737–766.

Collier, A. F., McClure, F. H., Collier, J., Otto, C., & Polloi, A. (1999). Culture-specific views of child maltreatment and parenting styles in a Pacific-Island community. *Child Abuse & Neglect, 23,* 2229–2244.

Committee on Ethical Guidelines for Forensic Psychologists, American Psychology-Law Society and Division 41 of the APA (1991). Specialty guidelines for forensic psychologists. *Law and Human Behavior, 15,* 655–665.

Condie, L. O. (2003). *Parenting evaluations for the court: Care and protection matters.* New York: Kluwer Academic/Plenum Publishers.

Conley, C. (2003–2004). A review of parenting capacity assessment reports. *Ontario Association of Children's Aid Societies, 47,* 16–23. Retrieved on March 8, 2009, from http://www.oacas.org/pubs/oacas/journal/2003_2004winter/2003_2004winter.pdf.

Connell, M. (2006). Notification of purpose in child custody evaluation: Informing the parties and their counsel. *Professional Psychology: Research and Practice, 37,* 446–451.

Conners, N. A., Whiteside-Mansell, L., Deere, D., Ledet, T., & Edwards, M. C. (2006). Measuring the potential for child maltreatment: The reliability and validity of the Adult Adolescent Parenting Inventory-2. *Child Abuse & Neglect, 30,* 39–53.

Cook County Juvenile Court Clinic (2008). *Training materials.* Unpublished manuscript.

Courtney, M. E., Barth, R. P., Berrick, J. D., Brooks, D., Needell, B., & Park, L. (1996). Race and child welfare services: Past research and future directions. *Child Welfare, 75,* 99–137.

Craig, R. J. (2006). The Millon Clinical Multiaxial Inventory-III. In R. P. Archer (Ed.), *Forensic uses of clinical assessment instruments* (pp. 121–145). Mahwah, NJ: Lawrence Erlbaum Associates, Publishers.

Crittenden, P. M., & Ainsworth, M. D. S. (1989). Child maltreatment and attachment theory. In D. Cicchetti & V. Carlson (Eds.), *Child maltreatment: Theory and research on the causes and consequences of child abuse and* neglect (pp. 432–463). Cambridge, U.K.: Cambridge University Press.

Darling, N., & Steinberg, L. (1993). Parenting style as context: An integrative model. *Psychological Bulletin, 113,* 487–496.

Daubert v. Merrell Dow Pharmaceuticals, Inc. (on remand), 43 F 3d1311 (1995).

Dozier, M., Peloso, E., Lindhiem, O., Gordon, M. K., Manni, M., Sepulveda, S., Ackerman, J., Bernier, A., & Levine, S. (2006). Developing evidence-based interventions for foster children: An example of a randomized clinical trial with infants and toddlers. *Journal of Social Issues, 62,* 767–785.

Dupuy v. McEwen, 495 F.3d 807 (7th Cir.), *cert. denied,* No. 07-1075 (U.S. 6/16/2008).

Dyer, F. J. (1999). *Psychological consultation in parental rights cases.* New York: Guilford Press.

Erard, R. D. (2007). Psychological testing and child custody evaluations in family court: A dialogue: Picking cherries with blinders on: A comment on Erickson et al. (2007) regarding the use of tests in family court. *Family Court Review, 45,* 175–184.

Erickson, S. K., Lilienfeld, S. O., & Vitacco, M. J. (2007). Psychological testing and child custody evaluations in family court: A critical examination of the suitability and limitations of psychological tests in family court. *Family Court Review, 45,* 153–170.

Eyberg, S. M., Nelson, M. M., & Boggs, S. R. (2008). Evidence-based psychosocial treatments for children and adolescents with disruptive behavior. *Journal of Clinical Child & Adolescent Psychology, 37,* 215–237.

Family Preservation and Support Initiative (1993). 42 U.S.C. P.L. 103-66, 107 Stat. 312 Part I § 13711 (1993), codified as amended, 42 USCA § 629 et seq.

Feerick, M. M., Knutson, J. F., Trickett, P. K., & Flanzer, S. M. (Eds.) (2006). *Child abuse and neglect: Definitions, classifications, and a framework for research.* Baltimore: Paul H. Brookes Publishing Co.

Fox, R. A. (1994). *Parent Behavior Checklist manual,* Austin, TX: Pro Ed.

Frye v. United States, 293 F. 1013 (D.C. Cir 1923).

Garb, H. N., Wood, J. M., Lilienfeld, S. O., & Nezworski, M. T. (2005). Roots of the Rorschach controversy. *Clinical Psychology Review, 25,* 97–118.

Gershoff, E. T. (2002). Corporal punishment by parents and associated child behaviors and experiences: A meta-analytic and theoretical review. *Psychological Bulletin, 128,* 539–579.

Goldstein, J., Freud, A., & Solnit, A. J. (1979). *Before the best interests of the child.* New York: Free Press.

Gray, E., & Cosgrove, J. (1985). Ethnocentric perceptions of childrearing practices in protective services. *Child Abuse & Neglect, 9,* 389–396.

Grisso, T. (1986). *Evaluating competencies: Forensic assessment and instruments.* New York: Plenum Press.

Grisso, T. (2003). *Evaluating competencies: Forensic assessments and instruments* (2nd ed.). New York: Kluwer Academic/Plenum Publishers.

Grisso, T., & Quinlan, J. (2005). Juvenile court clinical services: A national description. *Juvenile and Family Court Journal, 56,* 9–20.

Griswold v. Connecticut, 381 U.S. 479 (1965).

Guggenheim, M. (1995). The effects of recent trends to accelerate the termination of parental rights of children in foster care—An empirical analysis in two states. *Family Law Quarterly, 29,* 121–140.

Guidubaldi, J., & Cleminshaw, H. K. (1988). Development and validation of the Cleminshaw Guidubaldi Parent Satisfaction Scale. In M. J. Fine (Ed.), *The second handbook on parent education: Contemporary perspectives* (pp. 257–278). San Diego: Academic Press.

Haller, L. H. (2002). The forensic evaluation and court testimony. *Child and Adolescent Psychiatric Clinics of North America, 11,* 689–704.

Hansen, K. K. (1997). Folk remedies and child abuse: A review with emphasis on *caida de mollera* and its relationship to shaken baby syndrome. *Child Abuse & Neglect, 22,* 117–127.

Harkness, S., & Super, C. M. (Eds.) (1996). *Parents' cultural belief systems: Their origins, expressions, and consequences.* New York: Guilford Press.

Haskett, M. E., Scott, S. S., Willoughby, M., Ahern, L. & Nears, K (2006). The Parent Opinion Questionnaire and child vignettes for use with abusive parents: Assessment of psychometric properties. *Journal of Family Violence, 21,* 137–151.

Haskins, R., Wulczyn, F., & Webb, M. B. (2007). Using high-quality research to improve child protection practice. In R. Haskins, F. Wulczyn, & M. B. Webb (Eds.), *Child protection: Using research to improve policy and practice* (pp. 1–33). Washington, D.C.: Brookings Institution Press.

Hazan, A. L., Connelly, C. D., Kelleher, K. J., Landsverk, J. A., & Barth, R. P. (2007). Intimate partner violence in the child welfare system: Findings from the National Survey of Child and Adolescent Well-Being. In R. Haskins, F. Wulczyn, & M. B. Webb (Eds.), *Child protection: Using research to improve policy and practice* (pp. 44–61). Washington, D.C.: Brookings Institution Press.

Heilbrun, K. (2001). *Principles of forensic mental health assessment.* New York: Kluwer Academic/Plenum Publishers.

Heilbrun, K., Grisso, T. & Goldstein, A. M. (2009). *Foundations of forensic mental health assessment.* New York: Oxford University Press.

Heilbrun, K., Maraczyk, G., DeMatteo, D., & Mack-Allen, J. (2007). A principles-based approach to forensic mental health assessment: Utility and update. In A. M. Goldstein (Ed.), *Forensic psychology: Emerging topics and expanding roles* (pp. 45–72). Hoboken, NJ: John Wiley & Sons.

Heilbrun, K., Rogers, R., & Otto, R. K. (2002). Forensic assessment: Current status and future directions. In J. R. P. Ogloff (Ed.), *Taking psychology and law into the twenty-first century* (pp. 119–146). New York: Kluwer/Plenum.

Heilbrun, K., Warren, J., & Picarello, K. (2003). Third party information in forensic assessment. In A. M. Goldstein (Ed.), *Forensic psychology* (pp. 69–86), *Handbook of psychology, Vol. 11.* Hoboken, NJ: John Wiley & Sons.

Hong, G. K., & Hong, L. K. (1991). Comparative perspectives on child abuse and neglect: Chinese versus Hispanics and Whites. *Child Welfare, 70,* 463–471.

Hunsley, J., & Bailey, J. M. (1999). The clinical utility of the Rorschach: Unfulfilled promises and an uncertain future. *Psychological Assessment, 11,* 266–277.

Hurlburt, M. S., Barth, R. P., Leslie, L. K., Landsverk, J. A., & McCrae, J. S. (2007). Building on strengths: Current status and opportunities for improvement of parent training for families in child welfare. In R. Haskins, F. Wulczyn, & M. B. Webb (Eds.), *Child protection: Using research to improve policy and practice* (pp. 81–106). Washington, D.C.: Brookings Institution Press.

Hynan, D. J. (2003). Parent-child observations in custody evaluations. *Family Court Review, 41,* 214–223.

Idaho Code § 16-2005.

Ill. Comp. Stat. Ch. 705, § 405/1-2; Ch 750, § 50/1.

Indian Child Welfare Act of 1978. 25 U.S.C. P.L. 95-608.

Iowa Code § 232.111.

Jacobsen, T., Miller, L. J., & Kirkwood, K. P. (1997). Assessing parenting competency in individuals with severe mental illness: A comprehensive service. *Journal of Mental Health Administration, 24,* 189–199.

Jimenez, M. A. (1990). Permanency planning and the Child Abuse Prevention and Treatment Act: The paradox of child welfare policy. *Journal of Sociology and Social Welfare, 17,* 55–72.

Kan. Ann. Stat. §§ 38-2269; 38-2271.

Kauffman Best Practices Project (2004). *Closing the quality chasm in child abuse treatment: Identifying and disseminating best practices.* Charleston, SC: National Crime Victims Research and Treatment Center.

Kavanaugh, A., Clark, J., Masson, T., & Kahn, B. (2006). Obtaining and utilizing comprehensive forensic evaluations: The applicability of one clinic's model. *Nevada Law Journal, 6,* 890–912.

Keeping Children and Families Safe Act of 2003. P. L. 108-36, US HSS CB.

Kempe, C. H., Silverman, F. N., Steele, B. F., Droegemuller, W., & Silver, H. K. (1962). The battered-child syndrome. *Journal of the American Medical Association, 181,* 17–24.

Kerker, B. D., & Dore, M. M. (2006). Mental health needs and treatment of foster youth: Barriers and opportunities. *American Journal of Orthopsychiatry, 76,* 138–147.

Kirkland, K. (2003). A legal perspective on family psychology and family law: Comment on the special issue. *Journal of Family Psychology, 17,* 263–266.

Korbin, J. E. (1981). *Child abuse and neglect: Cross-cultural perspectives.* Berkeley: University of California Press.

Korbin, J. E. (1997). Culture and child maltreatment. In M. E. Helfer, R. S. Kempe, & R. D. Krugman (Eds.), *The battered child* (5th ed., pp. 29–48). Chicago: University of Chicago Press.

Kotchick, B. A., & Forehand, R. (2002). Putting parenting in perspective: A discussion of the contextual factors that shape parenting practice. *Journal of Child and Family Studies, 11,* 255–269.

Krauss, D. A., & Sales, B. D. (2003). Forensic psychology, public policy, and the law. In A. M. Goldstein (Ed.), *Handbook of psychology, Vol. 11: Forensic psychology* (pp. 543–560). New York: Wiley and Sons.

Kreeger, J. L. (2003). Family psychology and family law–a family court judge's perspective: Comment on the special issue. *Journal of Family Psychology, 17,* 260–262.

Krug, E. G., Dahlberg, L. L., Mercy, J. A., Zwi, A. B., & Lozano, R. (2002). *World report on violence and health.* Geneva: World Health Organization.

Kuehnle, K., Coulter, M., & Firestone, G. (2000). Child protection evaluations: The forensic stepchild. *Family and Conciliation Courts Review, 38,* 368–391.

Kuhmo Tire v. Carmichael, 526 U.S. 137 (1999).

Lally, S. J. (2003). What tests are acceptable for use in forensic evaluations? A survey of experts. *Professional Psychology: Research and Practice, 34,* 491–498.

Lansford, J. E., Chang, L., Dodge, K. A., Malone, P. S., Oburu, P., Palmérus, K., Bacchini, D., Pastorelli, C., Bombi, A. S., Zelli, A., Tapanya, S., Chaudhary, N., Deater-Deckard, K., Manke, B., & Quinn, N. (2005). Physical discipline and children's adjustment: Cultural normativeness as a moderator. *Child Development, 76,* 1234–1246.

Larzelere, R. E. (2000). Child outcomes of nonabusive and customary physical punishment by parents: An updated literature review. *Clinical Child and Family Psychology Review, 3,* 199–221.

Lee, S., Aos, S., & Miller, M. (2008). *Evidence-based programs to prevent children from entering and remaining in the child welfare system: Benefits and costs for Washington.* Olympia: Washington State Institute for Public Policy (Document No. 08-07-3901). Retrieved on January 08, 2009, from http://www.wsipp.wa.gov/pub.asp?docid= 08-07-3901.

Levesque, R. J. R. (2000). Cultural evidence, child maltreatment, and the law. *Child Maltreatment, 5,* 146–160.

Libby, A. M., Orton, H. D., Barth, R. P., & Burns, B. J (2007). Alcohol, drug, and mental health service need for caregivers and children involved with child welfare. In R. Haskins, F. Wulczyn, & M. B. Webb (Eds.), *Child protection: Using research to improve policy and practice* (pp. 107–119). Washington, D.C.: Brookings Institution Press.

Llewellyn, G., McConnell, D., & Ferronato, L. (2003). Prevalence and outcomes for parents with disabilities and their children in an Australian court sample. *Child Abuse & Neglect, 27*, 235–251.

Lutenbacher, M. (2001). Psychometric assessment of the Adult-Adolescent Parenting Inventory in a sample of low income single mothers. *Journal of Nursing Measurement, 9*, 291–308.

Maccoby, E. E., & Martin, J. A. (1983). Socialization in the context of the family: Parent-child interaction. In E. M. Hetherington (Ed.), *Handbook of child psychology* (Vol. 4, pp. 1–101). New York: Wiley.

Marchant, G. J., & Paulson, S. E. (2004). Review of the Parent-Child Relationship Inventory. *Mental Measurements Yearbook, 13* (accession no. 13121821).

Mason, M. A. (1994). *From father's property to children's rights: A history of child custody.* New York: Columbia University Press.

Medoff, D. (2003). The scientific basis of psychological testing: Considerations following Daubert, Kumbo, and Joiner. *Family Court Review, 41*, 199–212.

Melton, G. B., Petrila, J., Poythress, N. G., & Slobogin, C. (2007). *Psychological evaluations for the courts: A handbook for mental health professionals and lawyers* (3rd ed.). New York: Guilford.

Meyer, G. J., & Archer, R. P. (2001). The hard science of Rorschach research: What do we know and where do we go? *Psychological Assessment, 13*, 486–502.

Meyer v. Nebraska, 262 U.S. 390, 399 (1923).

Michigan Child Custody Act of 1970, §722.23 amended 1993.

Miller-Perrin, C. L., & Perrin, R. D. (2007). *Child maltreatment: An introduction.* Thousand Oaks, CA: Sage Publications.

Milner, J. S. (1986). *The Child Abuse Potential Inventory manual* (2nd ed.). DeKalb, IL: Psytec Inc.

Milner, J. S. (1990). *An interpretive manual for The Child Abuse Potential Inventory.* DeKalb, IL: Psytec, Inc.

Milner, J. S. (1994). Assessing physical child abuse risk: The Child Abuse Potential Inventory. *Clinical Psychology Review, 14*, 547–583.

Milner, J. S., & Crouch, J. L. (1997). Impact and detection of response distortions on parenting measures used to assess risk for child physical abuse. *Journal of Personality Assessment, 69*, 633–650.

Milner, J. S., Gold, R. G., Ayoub, C., & Jacewitz, M. M. (1984). Predictive validity of the Child Abuse Potential Inventory. *Journal of Consulting and Clinical Psychology, 52*, 879–884.

Moretti, M. M., Campbell, J., Samra, J., & Cue, B. (2003, July 7). *Empirical evaluation of parenting capacity assessments in British Columbia: Toward quality assurance and evidence based practice.*

British Columbia, Canada: Family Court Centre, Provincial Services, Ministry for Children and Family Development.

Myers, J. E. B. (2004). *A history of child protection in America.* Bloomington, IN: Xlibris.

Myers, J. E. B. (2006). *Child protection in America.* New York: Oxford.

Myers, J. E. B., Berliner, L. Briere, J., Hendrix, C. T., Jenny, C., & Reid, T. A. (Eds.) (2002). *The APSAC handbook on child maltreatment* (2nd ed.). Thousand Oaks, CA: Sage Publications.

National Children's Advocacy Center. (2005). *The child advocacy center model.* Retrieved from the National Children's Advocacy Center web site November 1, 2008, at www.nationalcac.org/professionals/ model/cac_model.html. Huntsville, AL: National Children's Advocacy Center.

National Maternal and Child Health Center for Child Death Review (2008). *Child Abuse and Neglect Fact Sheet.* Retrieved August 29, 2008, from http://www.childdeathreview.org/causesCAN. htm.

National Research Council and Institute of Medicine (2000). *From neurons to neighborhoods: The science of early childhood development.* Committee on Integrating the Science of Early Childhood Development. Jack P. Shonkoff and Deborah A. Phillips, eds. Board on Children, Youth, and Families, Commission on Behavioral and Social Sciences and Education. Washington, D.C.: National Academy Press. Retrieved March 8, 2009, from http://books.nap.edu/openbook.php?record_id=9824&page=R2.

New York Society for the Prevention of Cruelty to Children (2000). *The New York Society for the Prevention of Cruelty to Children 125th anniversary, 1875–2000.* Retrieved from the New York Society for the Prevention of Cruelty to Children web site July 4, 2008, at http:// www.nyspcc.org/beta_history/index_history.htm. New York: New York Society for the Prevention of Cruelty to Children.

Nicholson, J., Sweeney, E. M., & Geller, J. L. (1998a). Mothers with mental illness: I. The competing demands of parenting and living with mental illness. *Psychiatric Services, 49,* 635–642.

Nicholson, J., Sweeney, E. M., & Geller, J. L. (1998b). Mothers with mental illness: II. Family relationships and the context of parenting. *Psychiatric Services, 49,* 643–649.

Nilsen, W. J. (2003). Perceptions of attachment in academia and the child welfare system: The gap between research and reality. *Attachment & Human Development, 5,* 303–306.

NY CLS Soc Serv § 384-b.

Oberlander, L. B. (2002). Case 1: Principle: Obtain appropriate authorization. In K. Heilbrun, G. R. Marczyk, & D. DeMatteo (Eds.), *Forensic mental health assessment: A casebook* (pp. 350–375). New York: Oxford University Press.

Office of the Surgeon General (2000). Report of the Surgeon General's Conference on Children's Mental Health: A National Action Agenda.

Retrieved March 2, 2007, from http://www.hhs.gov/surgeonge-neral/topics/cmh/childreport.htm.

Ohio Rev. Code Ann. § 2151.414.

Ostler, T. (2008). *Assessment of parenting competency in mothers with mental illness.* Baltimore, MD: Paul H. Brookes Publishing Co.

Otto, R. K., & Edens, J. F. (2003). Parenting capacity. In T. Grisso, *Evaluating competencies: Forensic assessments and instruments* (2nd ed., pp. 229–307). New York: Kluwer/Plenum.

Otto, R. K., & Melton, G. B. (1990). Trends in legislation and case law on child abuse and neglect. In R. T. Ammerman & M. Hersen (Eds.), *Children at risk: An evaluation of factors contributing to child abuse and neglect* (pp. 55–83). New York: Plenum.

Pezzot-Pearce, T. D., & Pearce, J. (2004). *Parenting assessments in child welfare cases: A practical guide.* Toronto: University of Toronto Press.

Pierce v. Society of Sisters, 268 U.S. 510, 535 (1925).

Prince v. Massachusetts, 321 U.S. 158, 166 (1944).

Prinz, R. J., Sanders, M. R., Shapiro, C. J., Whitaker, J. D., & Lutzker, J. R. (2009). Population-based prevention of child maltreatment: The U.S. Triple P system population trial. *Prevention Science, 10*, 1–12.

Reder, P., & Lucey, C. (Eds.), (1995). *Assessment of parenting: Psychiatric and psychological contributions.* London: Routledge.

Reitman, D., Currier, R. O., & Stickle T. R. (2002). A critical evaluation of the Parenting Stress Index-Short Form (PSI-SF) in a Head Start population. *Journal of Clinical Child and Adolescent Psychology, 31*, 384–392.

Reynolds, A. J., Mathieson, L. C., & Topitzes, J. W. (2008). Do early childhood interventions prevent child maltreatment? A review of research. *Child Maltreatment, 14*, 182–206.

Roberts, D. (2002). *Shattered bonds: The color of child welfare.* New York: Basic Civitus Books.

Rogers, R., Salekin, R. T., & Sewell, K. W. (1999). Validation of the Millon Clinical Multiaxial Inventory for Axis II disorders: Does it meet the *Daubert* standard? *Law and Human Behavior, 23*, 425–443.

Rogosch, F. A., Cicchetti, Shields, & Toth, S. L. (2002). Parenting dysfunction in child maltreatment. In M. H. Bornstein (Ed.), *Handbook of parenting (Vol. 4): Applied and practical parenting* (pp. 127–159). Mahwah, NJ: Lawrence Erlbaum Associates, Publishers.

Rosenfeld, A. A., Altman, R., Alfaro, J., & Pilowsky, D. (1994). Foster care, child abuse and neglect, and termination of parental rights. *Child and Adolescent Psychiatric Clinics of North America, 3*, 877–893.

Rosenberg, S. A., Smith, E. G., & Levinson, A. (2007). Identifying young maltreated children with developmental delays. In R. Haskins, F. Wulczyn, & M. B. Webb (Eds.), *Child protection: Using research to improve policy and practice* (pp. 34–43). Washington, D.C.: Brookings Institution Press.

Rubin, D. M., O'Reilly, A. L. R., Hafner, L., Luan, X., & Localio, A. R. (2007). In R. Haskins, F. Wulczyn, & M. B. Webb (Eds.), *Child protection: Using research to improve policy and practice* (pp. 171–186). Washington, D.C.: Brookings Institution Press.

Sales, B. D., & Shuman, D. W. (1998). The admissibility of expert testimony based on clinical judgment and scientific research. *Psychology, Public Policy, and Law, 4*, 1226–1252.

Santosky v. Kramer, 455 U.S. 745, 752-754 (1982).

Sattler, J. M. (1998). *Clinical and forensic interviewing of children and families.* San Diego: Author.

Scally, J. T., Kavanaugh, A. E., Budd, K. S., Baerger, D. R., Kahn, B. A., & Biehl, J. L. (2001–2002). Problems in acquisition and use of clinical information in juvenile court: One jurisdiction's response. *Children's Legal Rights Journal, 21*, 15–24.

Schmidt, F., Cutress, L. J., Lang, J., Lewandowski, M. J., & Rawana, J. S. (2007). Assessing the parent-child relationship in parenting capacity evaluations: Clinical applications of attachment research. *Family Court Review, 45*, 247–258.

Sedlak, A. J., & Broadhurst, D. D. (1996). *Third National Incidence Study on child abuse and neglect.* Washington, D.C.: U.S. Department of Health and Human Services.

Shelton, K. K., Frick, P. J., & Wootton, J. (1996). Assessment of parenting practices in families of elementary school–age children. *Journal of Clinical Child Psychology, 25*, 317–329.

Skowron, E., & Reinemann, D. H. S. (2005). Effectiveness of psychological interventions for child maltreatment: A meta-analysis. *Psychotherapy: Theory, Research, Practice, Training, 42*, 52–71.

Social Services Block Grant, Title XX of the Social Security Act. (1975). 42 U.S.C.

Standards for Educational and Psychological Testing (1999). Washington, D.C.: American Psychological Association.

State ex rel. Watts v. Watts, 77 Misc. 2d 178, 350 N.Y.S. 2d 285. (1973).

Steele, B. F., & Pollock, C. B. (1968). A psychiatric study of parents who abuse infants and small children. In R. E. Helfer & C. H. Kempe (Eds.), *The battered child* (pp. 89–133). Chicago: University of Chicago Press.

Stredny, R. V., Archer, R. P., & Mason, J. A. (2006). MMPI-2 and MCMI-III characteristics of parental competency examinees. *Journal of Personality Assessment, 87*, 113–115.

Summers, A., Dobbin, S. A., & Gatowski, S. I. (2008). The state of juvenile dependency court research: Implications for practice and policy. Retrieved from National Council of Juvenile and Family Court Judges Website July 30, 2009, at http://www.ncjfcj.org/images/stories/dept/ppcd/pdf/juveniledependencybriefinal.pdf. Reno, NV: National Council of Juvenile and Family Court Judges, Permanency Planning for Children Department.

Taylor, C. G., Norman, D. K., Murphy, J. M., Jellinek, M., Quinn, D., Poitrask, F. G., & Goshko, M. (1991). Diagnosed intellectual and emotional impairment among parents who seriously mistreat their children: Prevalence, type, and outcome in a court sample. *Child Abuse & Neglect, 15*, 389–401.

Thorndike, R. L., Hagen, E. P., & Sattler, J. M. (1986). *Stanford-Binet Intelligence Scale, Fourth Edition: Technical manual.* Chicago, IL: Riverside.

Tippins, T. M., & Wittmann, J. P. (2005). Empirical and ethical problems with custody recommendations: A call for clinical humility and judicial vigilance. *Family Court Review, 43*, 193–222.

Troxel et vir. v Granville, 530 U.S. 57, 120 S.Ct. 2054 (2000).

U.S. Department of Health and Human Services (DHHS), Administration on Children, Youth and Families (2009). *Child Maltreatment 2007.* Washington, D.C.: U.S. Government Printing Office.

U.S. Equal Opportunity Employment Commission (1990). *Americans with Disabilities Act of 1990* (ADA) P. L. 101-336, 42 U.S.C. § 12101.

U.S. Government Accounting Office (2007) GAO-07-816, *African American children in foster care.* Retrieved July 19, 2008, from http://www.gao.gov/new.items/d07816.pdf.

Watkins, S. A. (1990). The Mary Ellen myth: Correcting child welfare history. *Social Work, 35*, 500–503.

Wechsler, D. (1992). *Wechsler Individual Achievement Test manual.* San Antonio, TX: Psychological Corporation.

Wechsler, D. (1999). *Wechsler Abbreviated Scale of Intelligence.* San Antonio, TX: Psychological Corporation.

Weiner, I. B. (1999). What the Rorschach can do for you: Incremental validity in clinical applications. *Assessment, 6*, 327–339.

Weiner, I. B. (2006). The Rorschach inkblot method. In R. P. Archer (Ed.), *Forensic uses of clinical assessment instruments* (pp. 181–207). Mahwah, NJ: Lawrence Erlbaum Associates, Publishers.

Weisz, J. R., Jensen-Doss, A., & Hawley, K. M. (2006). Evidence-based youth psychotherapies versus usual clinical care: A meta-analysis of direct comparisons. *American Psychologist, 61*, 679–689.

Whipple, E. E., & Richey, C. A. (1997). Crossing the line from physical discipline to child abuse: How much is too much? *Child Abuse & Neglect, 21*, 431–444.

Wildfire, J., Barth, R. F., & Green, R. L. (2007). Predictors of reunification. In R. Haskins, F. Wulczyn, & M. B. Webb (Eds.), *Child protection: Using research to improve policy and practice* (pp. 155–170). Washington, D.C.: Brookings Institution Press.

Wilson, S. R., Rack, J. J., Shi, X., & Norris, A. M. (2008). Comparing physically abusive, neglectful, and non-maltreating parents during interactions with their children: A meta-analysis of observational studies. *Child Abuse & Neglect, 32*, 897–911.

Wolfe, D. A. (1999). *Child abuse: Implications for child development and psychopathology* (2nd ed.). Thousand Oaks, CA: Sage Publications.

Wood, J. M., Nezworski, M. T., Garb, H. N., & Lilienfeld, S. O. (2001). The misperception of psychopathology: Problems with the norms of the Comprehensive System for the Rorschach. *Clinical Psychology: Science and Practice, 8*, 350–373.

W VA Code § 49-6-5b.

Yanez, Y. T., & Fremouw, W. (2004). The application of the *Daubert* standard to parental capacity measures. *American Journal of Forensic Psychology, 22*, 5–29.

Youth Law Center (2000). *Making reasonable efforts: A permanent home for every child.* Retrieved December 19, 2008, from http://www.ylc. org/pdfs/childrenmakingreason.pdf. San Francisco, CA: Youth Law Center.

Tests and Specialized Tools

BDI-II: Beck Depression Inventory II (Beck, Steer, & Brown, 1996)

BSI: Brief Symptom Inventory (Derogatis, 1993)

CAPI: Child Abuse Potential Inventory (Milner, 2004)

DPICS: Dyadic Parent-Child Interaction Coding System (Eyberg, Nelson, Duke, & Boggs, 2005)

HOME: Home Observation for the Measurement of the Environment Inventory (Caldwell & Bradley, 1984)

MCMI-III: Millon Clinical Multiaxial Inventory (Millon, 1997)

MMPI-2: Minnesota Multiphasic Personality Inventory 2 (Butcher, Graham, Ben-Porath, Tellegen, Dahlstrom, & Kaemmer, 2001)

PAI: Personality Assessment Inventory (Morey, 1991)

PASS: Parent Awareness Skills Survey (Bricklin, 1990)

PCRI: Parent-Child Relationship Inventory (Gerard, 1994)

PPCP: Parent Perception of Child Profile (Bricklin & Elliott, 1991)

PSI: Parenting Stress Index (Abidin, 1995)

SCL-90-R: Symptom Checklist 90-R (Derogatis, 1994)

SIPA: Stress Index for Parents of Adolescents (Sheras, Abidin, & Konold, 1998)

VABS-II: Vineland Adaptive Behavior Scales Second Edition (Sparrow, Balla, & Cicchetti, 2005)

WAIS-IV: Wechsler Adult Intelligence Scale–Fourth Edition (Wechsler, 2008)

Stanford-Binet-Revised

WRAT-3: Wide Range Achievement Test-3

References

Abidin, R. (1995). *Parenting Stress Index manual* (3rd ed.). Odessa, FL: Psychological Assessment Resources.

Beck, A. T., Steer, R. A., & Brown, G. K. (1996). *BDI-II manual.* San Antonio, TX: The Psychological Corporation.

Bricklin, B. (1990). *Parent Awareness Skills Survey manual.* Furlong, PA: Village Publishing.

Bricklin, B., & Elliott, G. (1991) *Parent Perception of Child Profile.* Furlong, PA: Village Publishing.

Butcher, J. N., Graham, J. R., Ben-Porath, Y. S., Tellegen, A., Dahlstrom, W. G., & Kaemmer, B. (2001). *Minnesota Multiphasic Personality Inventory-2 (MMPI-2): Manual for administration, scoring, and interpretation* (rev. ed.). Minneapolis: University of Minnesota Press.

Caldwell, B. M., & Bradley, R. H. (1984). *Home Observation for the Measurement of the Environment: Administration manual* (rev. ed.). Little Rock: University of Arkansas.

Derogatis, L. R. (1993). *Brief Symptom Inventory: Administration, scoring and procedures manual.* Minneapolis, MN: National Computer Systems Pearson.

Derogatis, L. R. (1994). *Symptom Checklist–90–R: Administration, scoring and procedures manual.* Minneapolis, MN: National Computer Systems Pearson.

Eyberg, S. M., Nelson, M. M., Duke, M., & Boggs, S. R. (2005). *Manual for the Dyadic Parent-Child Interaction Coding System* (3rd ed). Retrieved September 13, 2009 from http://pcit.phhp.ufl.edu/measures/dpics%20(3rd%20edition)%20manual%20version%203203.07.pdf

Gerard, A. B. (1994). *Parent-Child Relationship Inventory manual.* Los Angeles: Western Psychological Services.

Millon, T. (1997). *MCMI-III manual* (2nd ed.). Minneapolis, MN: National Computer System.

Milner, J. (2004). The Child Abuse Potential (CAP) Inventory. In M. J. Hilsenroth & D. L. Segal (Eds.), *Comprehensive handbook of psychological assessment, Vol. 2: Personality assessment* (pp. 237–246). Hoboken, NJ: John Wiley & Sons.

Morey, L. C. (1991). *Personality Assessment Inventory professional manual.* Lutz, FL: Psychological Assessment Resources.

Sheras, P. L., Abidin, R. R., & Konold, T. R. (1998). Stress Index for Parents of Adolescents: Professional manual. Odessa, FL: Psychological Assessment Resources.

Sparrow, S. S., Balla, D. A., & Cicchetti, D. V. (2005). *Vineland Adaptive Behavior Scales manual* (2nd ed.). Circle Press, MN: American Guidance Service.

Wechsler, D. (2008). *Wechsler Adult Intelligence Scale* (4th ed.). San Antonio, TX: Psychological Corporation.

Wilkinson, G. S., & Roberston, G. J. (2006). *Wide Range Achievement Test* (4th ed.). Lutz, FL: Psychological Assessment Resources.

Case Law and Statutes

Daubert v. Merrell Dow Pharmaceuticals (1995)

Dupuy v. McEwen (2008)

Frye v. United States (1923)

Griswold v. Connecticut (1965)

Kuhmo Tire v. Carmichael (1999)

Meyer v. Nebraska (1923)

Pierce v. Society of Sisters (1925)

Prince v. Massachusetts (1944)

Santosky v. Kramer (1982)

State ex rel. Watts v. Watts (1973)

Troxel et vir v. Granville (2000)

Adoption and Safe Families Act (ASFA, P.L. 105.89, 1997)

Adoption Assistance and Child Welfare Act (AACWA, 1980)

Child Abuse Prevention and Treatment Act

Illinois Adoption Act

Indian Child Welfare Act, enacted in 1978 (ICWA, P.L. 95-608)

Keeping Children and Families Safe Act (KCFSA) (2003, P. L. 108-36)

Oregon Compulsory Education Act (Oreg. Ls., 5259)

Social Services Block Grant, Title XX of the Social Security Act (1975)

Key Terms

Battered child syndrome: A term describing a combination of physical and other indicators that a child's internal and external injuries resulted from acts committed by a parent or caretaker.

Best Interests of the Child standard: The standard used by the court in decisions that affect a child, such as placement determinations, adoption, and apportionment of time and responsibility following dissolution of marriage or other parenting arrangements. Factors considered by the court in deciding the best interests of a child may include: the child's age, sex, and mental and physical health; the age, lifestyle, and mental and physical health of the parents; emotional ties between the parents and the child; the ability of the parents to provide the child with food, shelter, clothing, and medical care; any potentially negative effect of changing the status quo; and the child's preference. The Best Interests of the Child standard has been adopted by all jurisdictions in the United States.

Bonding or attachment assessment: Measurement of a young child's behavior in the presence, absence, and return of a caregiver under conditions that vary in stressfulness, in order to assess the caregiver–child relationship. Mary Ainsworth developed the "Strange Situation" procedure as a research measure to observe attachment relationships between a caregiver and children between the ages of 9 and 18 months.

Child maltreatment: Alternatively termed *child abuse and neglect*, this includes all forms of physical and emotional maltreatment, sexual abuse, neglect, and exploitation that result in actual or potential harm to the child's health, development, or dignity.

Child protective services (CPS): A generic term referring to any state's agency that investigates and provides services when child maltreatment is suspected. States may refer to the child protection agency by another term such as "department of child and family services."

"Compelling reason" clause: As used in the text, this phrase refers to reasons why termination of parental rights would not be in the child's best interest. The determination of compelling reasons is made on a case-by-case basis and may include, for example, the child's age and preference regarding termination, or documentation of a reasonable likelihood that the parent will comply with intervention to make it possible for the child to safely remain or return home.

Informed consent: An individual's consent for another person to engage in intervention that would otherwise constitute an invasion of the individual's privacy, after the individual has been fully informed of the nature and consequences of the proposed action, is competent to consent, and consents voluntarily. Informed consent is not necessary in court-ordered or statutorily mandated evaluations in criminal or delinquency cases, or when authorized by legal counsel for the individual.

Minimally adequate parenting: The "floor" of acceptable parenting that is sufficient to protect the safety and well-being of the child.

Parens patriae: A Latin term meaning "parent of his nation," in law this refers to the public-policy power of the state to intervene against an abusive or negligent parent, legal guardian, or informal caretaker, or to act as the parent of any child or individual who is in need of protection. *Parens patriae* recognizes that the government has a strong interest in the care and nurturing of children and others who cannot function independently.

Pro se: Latin for "for oneself" and referring to representing oneself in a court proceeding without an attorney.

Protective factors: Factors that protect or buffer a child against negative developmental outcomes; that is, factors that are likely to lead to the needs of the child being met, or characteristics that decrease the impact of abuse or neglect.

Risk factors: Factors that are known to be associated with or predictive of negative outcomes, factors that are likely to lead to the needs of the child not being met.

Tender Years Doctrine: A legal doctrine that was used in deciding child custody issues in family courts beginning in the late 19th century. The doctrine presumes that during a child's tender years (generally regarded as birth to 13), the child should be in the mother's custody. Some courts held that the Tender Years Doctrine violated the Equal Protection Clause in the Fourteenth Amendment of the U.S. Constitution. States have replaced this doctrine by the "Best Interests of the Child" doctrine.

Termination of parental rights (TPR): The ending of the legal relationship between a child and the child's biological or adoptive parents, either by voluntary relinquishment or involuntary severance. The parent whose parental rights have been terminated has no ongoing rights, privileges, duties, or obligations to the child (with the possible exception of responsibility for support arrears owed before parental rights were terminated).

Ultimate legal issue: The particular legal question facing the court, for example, whether a parent's rights should be terminated, whether unsupervised visitation with a child should be granted to a parent, or whether a permanency goal should be changed from "adoption" to "return home."

Index

Note: Page references followed by "*f*" and "*t*" denote figures and tables, respectively.

About the Authors

Karen S. Budd, Ph.D., is Professor of Psychology, Director of Clinical Training, and directs the Parent–Child Interaction Therapy Program at DePaul University in Chicago. She formerly directed a demonstration and research project at Cook County Juvenile Court on assessing parenting capacity in child protection cases. She has authored two books, conducts research on prevention and intervention programs for young children with disruptive behavior problems, and was a Fulbright Senior Scholar in Prague, Czech Republic.

Mary Connell, Ed.D., ABPP, is in independent practice and works primarily on cases involving suspected sexual abuse or sexual offenses in the military and civilian sectors. Having spent 15 years working with child protective services matters and focusing a great deal on assessment of children when child sexual abuse is alleged, she writes in the areas of child maltreatment and child sexual abuse, and on ethics in forensic practice and in other areas of the interface between psychology and the law.

Jennifer R. Clark, Psy.D., is Clinical Director for the Child Protection Division at the Cook County Juvenile Court Clinic and Assistant Professor at Northwestern University Feinberg School of Medicine in Psychiatry and Behavioral Sciences. She specializes in assessment of parenting capacity in child protection cases. She also provides training to judges and attorneys involved in child protection proceedings and consults with child welfare officials.

CPSIA information can be obtained
at www.ICGtesting.com
Printed in the USA